US-IRAN NUCLEAR DEAL: POWER DYNAMICS FOR IRAN AND SAUDI ARABIA

SAJID MAHMOOD KHAN

DEDICATION

This work is dedicated to all the peace lovers of world

CONTENTS

ACKNOWLEDGMENTS

I don't find suitable words to interpret my feelings to the Almighty Allah, whose favors and kindness was all the time with me, in completing this book successfully.

I am indebted to my best friend Mr. Inam Ullah whose guidance, advice and patience regarding my this writing has been immeasurable. I am grateful for his insightful comments and observations regarding my book. My sincere thanks to all faculty members of Quaid-i-Azam University Islamabad especially Dr. Mujeeb Afzal (SPIR), who like a compass, activated the magnets of curiosity, knowledge and wisdom in me.

Finally, I must express my very profound gratitude to Ms. Tanzeela Javed for providing me with unfailing support and continuous encouragement despite my busy life.. Last but not the least; I am thankful to my elder brother Mr. Akbar -e- Azam for his words of encouragement and motivation. This accomplishment would not have been possible without the help of people mentioned above.

Sajid Mahmood Khan

1 INTRODUCTION

The Middle Eastern region has great importance in international relations particularly in the prevailing political arena similar to that during the Cold War. This region also holds significance because of the multidimensional factors including immense richness in terms of oil, strategic location, Islamic extremism, nuclear issue etc. Saudi Arabia and Iran are two important states of the region having potential to be a regional hegemon. The Iranian revolution brought dominance of Shiite clergy with radical changes in the country and its foreign policy approach towards the Arab world that greatly molded the direction of its foreign policy priorities particularly toward the neighboring Arab states. The current military capability of Iran enables it to fetch a sense of vulnerability amongst its Arab neighborhood of leading military expeditions and the proxies in the Gulf region.(Cooper, 2011)

The fall of Shah led to the serious rift in the US- Iran relations. The US administration hoped for the improvement due to the presence of many moderates in the high offices. The attack on US embassy in Tehran made the situation worse, as the 66 officials of the embassy were held hostage for several months by pro-Khomeni masses. The US administration broke ties with Iran in April 1980 and attempted to rescue the hostages but failed. The Regan administration called Iran "state sponsor of terrorists" in January 1984 due to support for Hezbollah in Lebanon. The US remained engaged in several small clashes with Iran Navy in the Gulf to protect its oil interest during the period 1987-88. In January 1989 President George H.W Bush said, "good will begets good will" referring to authorities.(Wright, 2011) Actually, it was an offer to improve the relations in return for release of hostages. Apparently, Iran helped and released hostages by the end of October 1991, but relations remained unchanged.

After taking oath of President, the Clinton administration adopted the dual containment strategy to keep Iran and Iraq weak states. Clinton imposed sanctioned on Iran in 1995-96 due to Iran nuclear program and disturbing peace program in Middle East region. The Clinton Administration offer dialogue to them president Khatmi in May 1997 but denied by President Khatemi. George W.Bush was very tough on the issue of Iran and declared Iran "Axis of evil" including Iraq and North Korea. Iran nuclear progress was very concern of the US President Bush in his address stated that the US would be close ally to democratic and free Iran. The Obama administration developed political pressure to engage Iran in options to resolute issues pertaining to its nuclear program therefore; the Obama administration rebuilt the US-Iran relations and successfully implemented the Joint plan of action. Some officials are of the view that international diplomacy can help in addressing the international community concern regarding nuclear activities of Iran. (Fitzpatrick, 2015) The emergence of ISSI reduces distance between the USA and Iran despite of having hostile relations very first time after Iranian revolution of 1979. Both states have differences over many issues at regional and international level.

Before the JCPA, there were efforts from European nations to make Iran to bring its nuclear program to a state where it can be acceptable to the USA and Israel. These efforts have focused on short-term confidence building instead of providing a permanent bridge between Iran and west. A Joint plan of Action (JPA) was announced in September 2013 and as a result of successful diplomacy between Iran and P5+1, the deal was to eliminate stockpile of 20% enrich uranium for some relief in economic sanctions. The IAEA confirm the compliance of Iran in reports. The P5+1 and Iran negotiated on the deal to settle the issue between Iran and world community on April 2015 both the parties reached on framework and The Joint Comprehensive Plan of Action (JCPoA) was finalized on 14 July 2015.(Elasrag, n.d.)

Saudi Arabia is concerned that the US-Iran Nuclear deal would allow more flow of cash into Iran's economy, which means more money and power to Shiite proxies in the region i.e. Syria, Iraq, Lebanon, Yemen and Saudi Arabia itself. These proxies wars can escalate into regional conflicts between Iran and Saudi Arabia and imbalance existing balance of power. President Barack Obama said that the USA will "cut off Iran most likely paths to a (nuclear) bomb. Mr. John Kerry, Secretary of State of United States at the time, also said on many occasion that this agreement will help in making this region more safer place not only for Israel but also for other allies. The President of Iran expressed his satisfaction over the nuclear deal and said "No matter what interpretations are given, Iran's right to enrichment has been recognized". ("Breakout deal on Iran", 2015) The supreme leader of Iran who is most powerful figure in the politics of Iran also termed this deal as an "achievement" and "success" despite several objection and concerns raised by both Israel and Saudi Arabia.

The Joint comprehensive plan of Action between Iran and six (P5+1) negotiation power enhance the role of Iran in the region against traditional rivals. The US views sponsoring non-state actors by Iran a great threat to its interests in the region. The Iran Nuclear program perpetuates the situation and fear of the US increased. The US administration imposed economic sanction on Iran to discourage its nuclear program. The weak economic growth leads the people of Iran to elect a moderate leadership for its economic growth in Jun 2013. The new administration of President Hassan Rouhani negotiated regarding its Nuclear program with great power (P5+1) to break the deadlock and move forward. After showing inflexibility on the nuclear progress and suppressing protestor in 2009, the US administration adopted the policy of "two track strategy". The two-track strategy was focusing on strong economic sanctions and negotiating on nuclear progress. The sanctions imposed in 2010 and 2013 were widely supported by the international community.

The UN and the US sanctions play very important role in shaping Iran behavior and help in bring Iran's government at the table of negotiating. The US administration stated on many occasions that the US will engage with gulf countries and military option is one of the options available regarding Iran nuclear programs. The newly elected President in 2013 election brought up radical changes in the Iran. President Rouhani while addressing the UN General Assembly told the international community that the Supreme Leader has given him authority to negotiate the nuclear program with the world community including the USA. The relationships of Iran with Arab States, United States and Israel are based on distrust, hostility, and confrontation. The misleading information among the Arab states helps in shaping and making the world view and regional view of the states, which are sometimes based on false assumption and perception developed due to many factors.

US-IRAN NUCLEAR DEAL: POWER DYNAMICS FOR IRAN AND SAUDI ARABIA

The USA along with China, Russia, France, UK, and Germany (P5+1) imposed strong economic sanctions against Iran which crippled the Iranian economy. This reduced popularity of Mahmoud Ahmadinejad and he suffered a defeat in 2012 elections. (Mac Farquhar, 2012) After assuming office in 2013, Iranian President Hassan Rouhani reversed the policies of previous administration regarding the foreign policies. Hassan Rouhani struggled to reach an agreement with the USA on its nuclear program and sanctions, and despite strong Israeli resistance and impractical demands on 2 April 2015, P5 + 1 states reached on a framework of the nuclear deal. (Samore, n.d.)

 The Middle Eastern region is one of the important regions in global politics. This region is prone to regional and international conflicts due to ideological differences amongst the regional actors and competition for influence and economic interests. One of the objectives of Iranian Nuclear Program is its desire for regional hegemony. (Abulof, May 2014) The current US-Iran Nuclear deal is playing very important role in the dynamic regional balance of power. This US-Iran nuclear deal is reducing pressure on Iran from the US and western powers, which will lead to increase the economic and political strength of Iran not only at regional level but also at international level that will disturb the existing balance of power between Iran and Saudi Arabia. This study attempt to investigate the impact of this US-Iran Nuclear deal on balance of power between Saudi Arabia and Iran.

According to F. Gregory Gause that the Saudi Arabia and Iran are competing for influence in different states of the region i.e. Lebanon, Iraq, Palestine but now it's in the Syrian and Yemen region. They are the leading powers on each side of the sectarian divide that helps to fuel many of the region's conflicts. Iran is one of the important actors in the region due to its military strength, strategic importance and economic resources. Iran is struggling for gaining a major sphere of influence in the Arab world. (F. Gregory Gause, 2010)

The changing environment of Middle East that has altered the power structure of the Middle Eastern region has led to a changing political environment that has overwhelmingly altered the power structure as well. The prospects of the regional cooperation represent an opportunity for more consolidated leadership in the Gulf for both Saudi Arabia and Iran. The opinion current political and security discourse of action are yet not that adequate to keep up security in the region in longer-run, particularly after the US attack of Iraq in 2003, the issues of uncertainty are still prevalent in the concerned regional elements. The US intervention in the region under the slogan of War against Terror, specifically after the overthrowing the Saddam Hussein's regime, the power politics of the Gulf region has shifted once again. Consequently it affected the diplomatic relations between both countries.

The unexpected outcome of the USA involvement disturbed the balance of power between the nations in the region of Middle East. The ideological differences between different sects of the region including Sunni and Shia are increasing. The proxies' elements from both Sunny and Shia sides are also flaming the situations. This whole situation increases distrust not only between the regional actors but also between the West and its Arab allies.

The security dilemma between Iran and Saudi Arabia depicts the views that Saudi Arab is one of the most powerful country in the gulf region which is enjoying the status of regional hegemony. The regime of Saudi Arabia is trying to maintain the policy of Status quo in to maintain its influence in the region.

US-IRAN NUCLEAR DEAL: POWER DYNAMICS FOR IRAN AND SAUDI ARABIA

The Saudi Arabia is one of the countries that feel a great deal of threat against the security with regards to prevailing political and security dynamics within its own systems. Since the transformations of the Arab world, The Saudi Arabian regime attempted different options through different means to reduced the threats and the subsequent dangers of losing its hegemony in the region. Saudi Arabia is adopting different strategies and policies which have effects not only at domestic level but also at whole regional level. On the other hand the top leadership of the Iran is also very attentive and aware about the changes and shifting of Saudi Arabian polices in the region. Saudi Arabia is establishing a powerful block of its allies to counter Iranian influence in the region. All this makes security of Saudi Arabia directly proportional to the insecurity of Iran due to their competing interests. (Hossein Salavatian, 2015)

One of the authors Paul N. Schwartz believes that may other states other than the Iran are beneficiaries of the nuclear deal with international powers. Including Russia, many other Western countries will also draw advantages out of this nuclear deal and consequently, the intra-state relationship will further improve. The international efforts for the resolution of Iranian nuclear crisis ultimately brought up a mutually agreed framework for easing the economic sanctions on Iran based on the conditions that Iran would limit the production of plutonium and the enrichment of the uranium. Following the issues of agreement on the nuclear deal and Iran's relationship with the West, the Russian Federation will going have a unique role in the current political affairs of the Middle Eastern region. The permanent members of Security Council (United States, France, China, Russia, and the United Kingdom) along with Germany have engaged Iran through diplomacy which led to a successful accord between these permanent five members and Germany. The agreement sign on 30 June

2015 will limit the Iran nuclear programme and in return Iran will receive some predefined benefits from United Stated as well as different other actors, which also included economic benefit. The uplift of sanctions will not only beneficial for the west but it will also help Russia to enhance its role and economic power. It shows that the relation of Iran with Russia and western countries will be improve and will gain economic benefits as a result of this deal to strengthen their economy. (Schwartz, 2015)

The writers of *"Iran's security policy in the post-revolutionary era"* published by RAND, which assesses Iran's security policy that describe the Tehran security policy and design for regional hegemony, instigated Tehran to forge ties to a variety of Islamist movements and, at times, it also struggles to promote the policy of creating such militia groups. Iran is denying any direct involvement for proxies and militants in different countries around the Middle Eastern region including Iraq, Yemen and Saudi Arabia despite of its support for different Islamist and revolutionary elements struggling for influence and dominance in the mentioned countries. (Daniel Byman, 2001)

Dr. Nader Entessar writes about the reasons of Saudi Arabia's concerns over Iran nuclear program and the political and economic gains after successful results of the Iran and P5+1 states of the world. The dilemmatic reasons following Iran's nuclear program is one of the main issues for regional instability and disturbance of the power equilibrium. The nuclear program of Iran started on 5 March 1957 after the Shah had signed the 'Atoms for Peace' Program, a United States' initiative to promote peaceful nuclear development in the world. The other scenario erupting after the success of the deal will help Iran in gaining momentous in terms of political and economic superiority that is however, unacceptable to many states in the region including Saudi Arabia. (Entessar N., Summer 2015)

US-IRAN NUCLEAR DEAL: POWER DYNAMICS FOR IRAN AND SAUDI ARABIA

Faisal bin Salman al-Saud author of book "Iran, Saudi *Arabia and the Gulf: Power Politics in Transition"* is of the view in his book that the regional balance of power in the late 1960s and early 1970s calls for a focus on Iran's role. The wars and prolong conflicts have significantly contributed to the economic and military growth of many states in the region and Iran has been one of those which following the years of Gulf war has effectively built-up its power, position and national growth. (Faisal bin S.al-Saud 2008). Iran is the only power in the region, which can utilized its resources and political influence to become regional hegemony with sufficient power to significantly alter the political scenario of Middle Eastern region. Iran has been sacrificing most of its vital goals of national interest. (Al-Saud, 2003)

Right from the days of Islamic revolution though Iran faced political isolation and economic sanctions and has survived to cope with the challenges arising with time to time. Iraq as a first Shiite dominated state is the political achievement of Iran. According to Barry Rubin, Iran is enhancing its role in different parts or the region including , Afghanistan, Iraq, Lebanon etc through various groups backed by it. Iran is constantly

maximizing its role in the region.

Iran's involvement is essential to the Assad regime's ability to survive and continue his rule. In contemporary Arab world, the most persistent meddler is not the USA or the West, but Iran. In Lebanon, the Iranians are supporting Hezbollah as a state within a state. In Yemen, the Iranians provided assistance to the Houthi rebellion in the north. In the two worst conflicts in the Arab, world - in Iraq and Syria - Iran is an important player. The blazing sectarian battles that have engulfed Iraq sparked since the US invasion - but the fuel has come in large part from Iran. (Yafai, 2013)

Dr. Barzegar Kayhan is of the view that the contemporary situation and actions greatly affect the power equilibrium. Moreover, the Washington considers Iran's action responsible for bringing insecurity to the region whereas, Tehran regards those as bringing security to the region while the USA and Arabs states consider the measures of Iran for security enhancing are threat to regional balance of power. United States and Iran are working to establish new security arrangements, which will not only be accommodating to the USA but also to Iranian interests in the region. The joint security arrangements and cooperation between Tehran and Washington will ensure the advancement of common interests. The regional political and security matters call for a cooperative role between Iran and the United States to tackle all the issues that are beyond the control of any single state to handle individually. (Barzegar, 2010)

One of the book written by Louise Fawcett having title *"International Relations of the Middle East"* which explains the international relation of Middle East, it covers historical and some contemporary trends in International Relations of Middle East. The author explains in the book that oil is one of the variant factors amidst Arab and Gulf states' the relationship. The role of black gold (petroleum oil) is very crucial not only in the regional but also in the international affairs, especially for the industrial countries, which are badly in need of Middle Eastern oil to run their machinery.

Many states are struggling to dominate the economic resources such as previously controlling the trade and now it has become the issue of dominating the oil and natural gas resources, even the less industrialized states of the region depend on oil and consider it as one of the important commodities not only for the economy of Middle East but also for regional and international politics. (Fawcett, 2013)

US-IRAN NUCLEAR DEAL: POWER DYNAMICS FOR IRAN AND SAUDI ARABIA

The foremost challenge for Iran was a security threat posed by the Saddam Husain's regime but current situation in Iraq has enabled Iran to compete against the Saudi dominance without fears of thread from any other state in the region. Apart from the conventional military means, the nuclear program for Iran is gaining its influence on the region. Ms. Saira Khan examined about the force behind the nuclear program in the region, she is of the opinion that Iran is endeavoring for its historic pride after defeat of Iraq. The nuclear programme of Iran is one of the option available with Iran to regain its role in the region. On the other hand Saudi Arabia is threaten by the expansionists ambitions of Iran, which is challenging Saudi Arab hegemony. After such ambitious of Iran for enhancing its role and hegemony could possibility lead to escalation of tension between Iran and other regional great power especially Saudi Arabia. In this book Ms. Saira tells the importance of nuclear program for Iran to gaining its influence on the region. (Khan, 2010)

Hooshang Amirahmadi says that there are three main factors which are the main reason of hostile relations between Iran and Suadi Arabia. These factors included the religious and ideological differences, differences between Arab and Persian cultures, and a desire for regional hegemony and influence in the Middle Eastern region including a most dominant role for leading the oil producing countries. (Entessar H. A., 1993)

According to Lina Haddad Kreidie, describing the rise of Iran and response by Saudi government with different means. The contested interpretation of different religious ideologies and history by Saudi Arabia and Iran through their scholars, journalists, religious clerics and different madrasa to heighten their religious and ideological superiority and infuse sectarianism to counter the Iranian's identity, which is Shiite identity influenced by Persian culture.

These contesting ideas and confrontations at different fronts can be seen evidently in contemporary international relations of Middle east. The current evolving violent ideologies in the region are security threats to the different regional actors. These interpretations of ideas are evolving through different proxies lead by the main actors as well as other international actors. The Arab spring also change the political scenario of the Middle Eastern region. The Saudi Arabian army movement toward Bahrain for securing it against any aggression and plot backed by Iranian is also one of the possible insecurity felt by the Royal regime in Saudi Arabia. The Saudi-Iran competition for the region's dominance has engaged a variety of means such as clerics, opinion makers, media and many other tools of propagation of their respective religious and sectarian ideology since both consider it an effective means to hold an influential position in the regional affairs. The volatile region is also one of the threat to status quo of Saudi Arabia in the region. (Lina Haddad Kreidie, November, 2013)

The lifting of sanctions on Iranian economy is having its affects and all economic indicators are moving in a positive direction which ensures its prospective position having sound economic and military power to manage and pursue a nuclear program whenever it needed. According to one of the Saudi researcher (Mansor al Marzoki)while talking to Al Jazera News, he said that Saudi Arabia views this deal as an attempt to boost Iranian economy, which will ultimate lead to insecurity to Saudi Arabia and the region. This deal is seen as attempt by Iran to gain more time for developing its nuclear programme. Saudi Arabian is of the opinion that this deal will not strike at the Iran's nuclear installation and sites.

According to the Press Release, No. 15/581 of International Monitory Fund IMF released on 21 December 2015 clearly stated that after the lifting of sanctions on Iranian economy it is growing and all economic indicators are moving in a positive direction. Its access to foreign assets will help in improving its GDP growth in future. The oil production and its revenue in terms of trading with the international community is reducing pressure on the stagnant economy. (IMF Country Report 15/349, 2015) Although the US-Iran nuclear deal restrict nuclear activities of Iran in the region but it will not resolve all outstanding issues of Iran with other states. This deal will increase the economic and political influence of Iran in the region. Iran will not receive the fruit of this deal until the implementation of joint comprehensive plan of action and dismantling its nuclear weapon capability. (Nader, 2015)

There are three major types of sanctions on Iran which are :-

a.   United Nations sanctions

b.   United States sanctions

c.   European Union and some allied countries sanctions

UN sanctions are primarily focusing on the nuclear program and other weapon of mass destruction program rather energy sector, trade, banking etc for development and humanitarian purpose. The resolution 1929-ban members countries to sell major weapon to Iran including Jet plan, Tanks, Missiles, Ships etc. The Resolution No. 1747 bans on Iran for exporting its arms to other entities, which mostly related with its military support to Hezbollah, Hamas and Shiite groups fighting in Iraq and Syria.

The US government banned firms for trading and investment with Iran except food and medical items The US administration banned foreign firm doing business / transactions with Iran in its energy sector. Iran is in the US list of state sponsoring terrorism for which any type of foreign assistance banned except humanitarian. The US imposed sanction on Iran regarding arms exports, shipping, banking etc Japan and Korea banned long term and medium term trade with Iran but short term transitions are allowed for civilian items. EU banned all types of trade with energy sector of Iran. EU also banned all types of aid, assistant and loan to Iran and those firms associated with Iran energy sector, banned all types of weapon sell to Iran including medium and short-range weapons. (Katzman, 2016)

According to an overview by World Band, Iran and Saudi Arabia are two major economic power based on hydrocarbon economies. Iran is the second largest country after Egypt in the Middle East and North Africa, dependent mainly on its oil revenues and to some extent on other sector like agriculture, services, manufacturing etc.

Currently Iran is very committed to it 6th five year plan (2016-21) based on the progress of the following three main areas.

    a) Development of Economy

    b) Science and Technology

    c) Culture

They have set different targets to achieve their vision. The yearly Economic Growth target is 8%, which is higher than previous years, utilization of Oil's income for the development of different sectors after achieving a successful nuclear deal with the US. After the President Rouhani taking charge as a president in July 2013 and successful agreement between P5+1 and Iran, the economy of Iran is on the right track to progress. The nuclear deal helps in uplifting sanction imposed by EU. UNO and the USA on Iran regarding Oil exports, account access, international banking etc. Because of this deal, Iran will able to promote and expand its economy in all directions including financing, banking, tourism etc. ("Iran Overview", 2016) Saudi

US-IRAN NUCLEAR DEAL: POWER DYNAMICS FOR IRAN AND SAUDI ARABIA

Arabia has instability at domestic as well as at international level due to anarchy in the region, whether it is Bahrain, Yemen, Syria or Iraq. The domestic stability and risk to the regime is link with stability in the region the external threats i.e. pan-Islamic movements ,Houthi uprising , Shia influenced organization etc are serious challenges for Saudi Arabia which can create panic and topple the regime specially after decline of Saudi Arabia economy due to lower prices of oil in international market . The trans-national ideologies and organization could possibly challenge the internal security of Saudi Arabia and challenge hegemony of Saudi Arabia internally and externally in the region.

Saudi Arabia perceived Iran presence as competition for regional dominance , Saudi Arabia view the Arab Spring and the US led invasion of Iraq as an action of destabilize the region which shift the existing power arrangements in favor of Iran . Saudi Arabia want to contain the spread of Iranian influence in the Arab world, this led the Saudi Arabia to behave aggressively on the different occasion i.e. Bahrain, Yemen, Syria etc.Saudi Arabia stress on the need to arm Syrian opposition forces and to counter the Iranian influence in the region and maintain a balance power. In the beginning, Saudi Arabia and Washington were working together against Assad regime. Saudi Arabia was uncomfortable after the refusal of the US air strikes and military operation in response to allegedly chemical weapon used by Assad regime against civilian. The removal of President Saleh from power was a serious blow to the efforts of Saudi Arabia to maintain its influence on Yemen. After realization the weak position of President Saleh, Saudi Arabia was looking for such a way, which may less effect the existing power equation in the region. The Houthi forces maximize their strength with the help of Iranian support and challenge the status quo maintain by Saudi Arabia. The US invasion of Iraq create power vacuum in the region, which led the insecurity for Saudi Arabia, this event persuade the new polices with respect to new dynamics. (Saudi Arabia: Putting on a brave face–Analysis, 2015)

The Joint Comprehensive Plan of Action (JCPA) is an agreement between Iran and six powers that is the USA, UK, China, Russia, France, and Germany. Its need arose due to insistence of Iran to enrich Uranium for nuclear energy purpose to a level that can be presumably used in the nuclear weapons as well. This uranium enrichment was considered unacceptable by Israel, which was constantly under harsh threatening criticism by Iranian political leadership due to Israeli unfair treatment of Palestinians. More, Iran has already been openly supported Hezbollah which is fighting Israel in Lebanon. Israel has been threatening to attack Iranian nuclear facilities preemptively similar to Operation Opera in which Israel destroyed Iraqi nuclear reactor on 7 June 1981. Israeli Air Force has been conducting military exercises of the attacks for several years. the USA feared that the Israeli attack on Iranian nuclear facilities would destabilize the whole Middle East region and consequently jeopardize world economy due to the dependency of world on Middle Eastern energy resources and Strait of Hormuz.

Iran has ratified the NPT (Treaty on the Non-Proliferation of the Nuclear Weapons) which grants Iran the right to enrichment of uranium for peaceful nuclear power generation. On the other hand Israel is keeping an ambiguous position on its nuclear weapon program and has not ratified the NPT. It is commonly believed that it has developed a large stockpile of the nuclear weapons along with highly reliable delivery systems with extensive technical and financial support from the USA, UK and France. Iran claims that it considers the nuclear weapons against their ideology of Islamic teachings due to their ability to spread mass destruction but on the other hand the USA claims that Iran can't be trusted to keep up with the agreement of NPT and not use the enriched uranium for weapons.

To stop Israel from attacking Iran, the USA needed to either stop Iran or limit its capabilities of uranium enrichment. For this purposes the USA first tried to threaten Iran with military attacks similar to Iraq war of 2003 but it faced harsh resistance from the international community for lying to the world even about Iraqi WMD. Then the USA imposed financial and economic sanctions against Iran by forcing other countries and institutions all over the world to stop financial and economic dealing with Iran. This badly affected Iranian Economy and contributed a lot in increased unemployment, inflation and higher poverty levels, but did not stop it from its progression of nuclear program very soon. In the mean time, other major powers like China and Russia and some other European nations felt that their economy was also being hurt. They kept pressure on both the USA and Iran to come up to negotiation table. This led to several phases of talks between the USA and Iran. In the meantime, Iran and Saudi Arabia were trying their best to disrupt the talks through using their influence in the Republican Party in the US Congress.

The internal community's notice on Iran's alleged nuclear weapons ambitions is soaring, but Tehran's deferred admittance and sustained manipulation with the International Atomic Energy Agency (IAEA) may, in the average to prolong, set aside Iran to squash ahead with a underground nuclear weapons program. Iran most likely glances to the Pyongyang's sculpt in which superficially kowtowed to the NPT and politically disseminate every international or the US determination of preventative military action to stalk the North Korean nuclear program. Subsequent to setting up a nominal nuclear disincentive, since North Korea was able to overtly vacate from the NPT and proclaim its nuclear weapons ambitions to up the pledge for any contemplation of the US-prompted military move against the recluse state. Iran also can view more rapidly around Iraq's ineffective proffer for nuclear weapons ambitions amidst the Gulf war. Iraq handled to stay in reasonable eminence with the NPT, despite the fact that wharfing a massive nuclear weapons setup that would have twisted a nuclear arsenal if it had not aggravated the US-led military intrusion with Saddam Husain's move of invading Kuwait. The examples from such experiences undermine for Tehran the possibility to carry on functioning on nuclear program besides the occurrence of IAEA inspections. WE obsessions with Iraq may sustain the Iranian poise about pursuance of a furtive nuclear weapons program below the vigilant sight of IAEA. The US political authenticity also is overwrought above the way of its recent engagements in Afghanistan and Iraq. Furthermore, the domestic and international perception about the reliability of the US intelligence is on qualm after an actually less productive move against Iraq and prompts a less provoked thought about harsh move against its nuclear weapons program. However, in a longer perspective a controversial stance on the nuclear program by Iranian leadership put the country in delicate situation. The political solution of such matter is inevitable for the best interest of Iran.

The dilemma of unreceptive relationship towards the Arab states traditionally undermines any international effort for a nuclear deal with Iran particularly due to the prevalent status-quo in the Persian Gulf and Middle Eastern region. During the Iraq-Iraq war, most of the Arab states politically, economically, and militarily backed Saddam Husain because a military success could lead to Iran's prospective strategically strong footholds in the Kuwait and Saudi Arabia. In addition, such a military edge in the region would have encouraged any possible adventure by Iranian side to promote its revolutionary fanaticism beyond the borders of the modest Arab states and dominate the regional balance of power. However, at that time, the Iran-Iraq war exceptionally exhausted the Iranian power and condensed the intensity of concern and threat perception in the Arab world. The US military presence in the region significantly generates a sense of fortification for the Arab states assuring to monitor and deter any military ambitions and dissuade any military adventure to upset the existing regional balance of power. Whereas, such a feeling of security by many Arab states turns onto the stake in course of a successful nuclear deal between Iran and the world powers. (Henry Sokolski and Patrick Clawson, 2005)

The current engagement of Iran in the regional security matters of its allies in Lebanon, Syria, Yemen and Iraq are incessantly shattered towards uncertainty. The delicate economic and political position of Iran will significantly stirrup after the successful outcomes of the US-Iran nuclear deal and will improve its position along with its allies in the region although disposing of the hopes of Arab allies and partners of the US in the region. The militant groups like Hezbollah who mainly get support from Iran indicate the outcomes of the Iran-US nuclear deal to support and put their axis in a stronger and better position locally and regionally ever before. Similarly, the Bashar Assad regime in Syria persists on sustaining by with the Iranian military, financial and political support. Because of the successful Iranian nuclear deal with the US and the international community there will be tremendous political gains that promising Iran's geopolitical victory but proves to be severe drawback for the Arab states of the region. Moreover, the politically and economically sound Iran also ensures the existence of Basha-ul-Assad's regime in Syria. Likewise, the militant groups like Hezbollah will also continue to obtain exceptional gains as a result of a successful nuclear deal between Iran and international powers.

For Arab states, a successful nuclear deal between Iran and the world powers does not merely compact with other grim intimidations but also enhances Iran's military capabilities and its agenda of supporting the proxies in the region. Iran has been financing, arming and training the militias operating in the countries around the Arab world. Furthermore, the Arab states view Hezbollah as one of Iran's largest forces that significantly continues to receive approximately over $1 billion annual funding from Iran. With such huge finances to maintain a militant group equipped with latest weaponry and even missile system, Iran needs not to directly indulge with any of Arab state but to exploit its proxy power in the region. The Iranian influence is further spreading in Iraq, Syria, Yemen, and Lebanon by managing and training other militia groups like Badr, Al-Mokhtar and Houthi groups.

For several years, the Islamic Republic of Iran has made America a mark of its acrimony by promoting anti-US sentiments in the country and to some extent successfully exacerbated such propagation in the region by creating hostile sentiments for the US and its allies. The general views hold the US and its allies responsible and a culprit behind every evil in the region however, with a feasible deal with the US, Iran has modified the mark of its loath avoiding the US and its Western allies' rage. Such an approach actually could promote their affairs to counterfeit sound relationship with the West. The Iranian regime's expression has been exercising a greater influence through its likeminded religious scholars and followers in the countries like Iraq, Syria and Lebanon and significant contribute in increasing the level of Shiite sectarian voice in the region. This emphasizes the views held by Arab world about Iran's anti-Sunni bloc intending on outlining an Iran-led Shiite factions for a closer religious-political association. Whereas, Hezbollah has already pledged to remain in Syria as long as the war against rebels and the ISIS ends. This strongly supports the fact the Hezbollah's recent intrusion on behalf of Iran to support Bashar-ul-Assad's regime in Syria has twisted a fresh gesture of sectarianism in the whole region. The pro-Iranian regime of Iraqi Prime Minister Maliki has significantly contributed in the face of Shiite dominance of Iraq.

The Iranian support to Prime Minster Maliki to tackle Al-Qaeda and other militant elements and the shore up rendered through using Iraqi territory for assisting Asad regime in terms of men and military equipment supply to Syria is another issue of concern for the neighboring Arab states.

This apprehension of Arab states due the prospect of Iran becoming nuclear power leads to an unending race for the procurement of the arms arsenal in the Middle Eastern region, where each state trying its level best to counter the threats arising from the hostile side. The only viable option with the international community is to check on the nuclear programme of Iran under the supervision of IAEC and UN watch dog. The check on Iran nuclear programme will not only control the arms race, but it will also enhance the security of region.

Iran could follow the suite on the similar grounds that it had a due right to safeguard its national security against any threat emanating from the belligerent state sitting in its immediate neighborhood or region. The Israeli authorities adopted the policy of ambiguity regarding its nuclear program.

The regional security implication encourage Israel to maintain its security through every means at any cost whereas, a nuclear capable Iran that has been constantly posing threats to Iran with the dire consequence and total elimination from the world map further add to the regional security dilemma.

To explore the state's behavior that could become the driving motive or intent for acquiring the nuclear weapons in their book, "The Spread of Nuclear Weapons: An Enduring Debate", the exceptionally convincing argument is about the flaws in international political system that pushes the states towards the nuclear option. Their argument proposes three core motives behind state's quest for the nuclear weapons namely, prestige, security and internal compulsions. However, the study leaves behind many unanswered question that were subsequently also suggest that no theory convincingly addresses the question of why states actually tries to acquire the nuclear weapons. The nuclear weapons have spread gradually and because they are difficult to develop and maintain, therefore, only a handful of countries would like these to be possessed which creates a balancing order as these serves as an extremely useful mechanism of deterring the war. The neo-realist theory that posits that distribution of power in the international system dictates state's behavior. Therefore, the more power a state acquires the more violent behavior it would adopt, which could only be tamed by a demonstrated mechanism of power in equal proportion, which consequently balances the structure or equation. The opinion that although the nuclear weapons are meant for deterrence, but there is no guarantee that these could or would never be used. According to Sagan, states sometimes resort to behaviors which can neither be termed rational nor proportionate to some given circumstances and thus could lead to situation which might involve use of the nuclear weapons.

There are certain organizational structures and mechanisms, which have their own interests, standard operating procedures, and customs that sometimes could remain outside the control of the political leadership, and therefore an accidental or an unauthorized use of the nuclear weapons would always remain a possibility. Their views present readers with logic and arguments to make their own conclusions that whether more states with the nuclear weapons would present a stable geo-political order or would lead to further instability. Moreover, the views provide an understanding of the various issues that warrants introspection while evaluating the effects of the nuclear weapons on regional and global stability. It elaborates the critical reviews of two opposing schools of thought regarding the spread of the nuclear weapons.

A similar critique of the realists' and the idealists' position on the nuclear proliferation help understanding the role and state's motivation for acquiring the nuclear weapons including that of the Middle Eastern states certain fragile security regional dynamics must be kept in view. Moreover, an influencing argument about nuclear pessimists and the nuclear optimists is issue of constant debate about the nature and role of the nuclear weapons in foreign policy objective attainment. To some levels, the nuclear weapon have contributed towards the global stability or is actually a recipe for a disaster waiting just for a right opportune, which may befall anytime in an anarchic world order.

One of the most critical factors in Iranian power struggle is creating a balance of power against Israel, since the Iranian clergy regards Israel as a foremost threat to its national security second to threats emanating from the US side. Despite maintaining an ambiguous posture over its nuclear program, the world clearly knows that Israel possesses the nuclear weapons. Furthermore, the Israeli nuclear capability remains the driving force behind the Iranian desire to pursue the quest for developing the nuclear weapons. (Sagan and Waltz 2003)

The Iranian participation in regional power structure creates a level of anxiety for the security of Saudi Arabia that also tries to expend and exercise greater influence over neighboring states and the domination of the whole region. Nevertheless, historically both Iran and Saudi Arabia successfully managed to sustain good relations before Islamic Revolution in Iran. The two states have remained some of most important strategic allies of the United States. However, the scenario drastically shifted after the Shah overthrown in 1979. Following the Revolution, the Saudi leadership also perceived a threat emanating from the Ayatollah Khomenei's spread of radical dogma based on Shiite ideology. The Arab world started assuming that the Khomenei's philosophy will expand towards the condemnation of the Sunni monarchies as adversative to Islam and his aspiration will export the impact of Iranian revolution to the rest of the Muslim world. As a counter measure, the Saudi Arabia and its Arab partner states enthusiastically supported Iraq's war against Iran in 1980 and supposed the Iraq will eventually roll back all the influence of revolutionary consequence of Tehran within the course of decisive war. Iraq got exceptional support from the Arab world for its stance over Iranian expansionism until the US-led invasion of Iraq in 2003. Similarly, the Saudi Arabia opted for a variety of options including those under the common agenda of the Gulf Cooperation Council (GCC), for raising a regional Arab alliance against expanding influence of Iran. (Latham 2011)

The recent history of Iranian foreign policy depicts a set particularly emphasizing 20th century goals for the nation and partners in the region. It draws a link between various events on the political horizon that have a direct bearing or linkage with the Iranian nuclear program. In this context, the famous CIA coup, which deposed the democratically elected Prime Minister of Iran, Mr. Mussadiq, paved the way for the Iranian monarch

Reza Shah Pahlavi, and proved to become as water shed event in the historic of modern Iran. Furthermore, with the end of the Cold War, the United States needed a pro-American regime in Iran that could provide it as an operating base for covert operations. Therefore, the US premier intelligence agency instigated to dismiss an elected leader to install an emperor that could serve in the best interests of the US in the region. Another very important reason for the CIA coup, according to author it was the oil factor. In the course of Gulf war, Iran alleged the US for providing the Saddam regime with chemical weapons to be used against Iran. Iran also brought the matter to the United Nations seeking for a resolution condemning the use of such weapons, which was blocked by the US. The uncertain security circumstances pushed Iran to pursue the path of acquiring the nuclear weapons program and counter any such threat in the future. (Patrikarakos 2012)

Although most of the states' clandestine nuclear programs were initiated through, the blessing opportunity provided by the Eisenhower administration five decades ago under the slogan of atom for peace program in order to utilize nuclear technology for peaceful purposes and benefited many new states in the world for their quest for nuclear technology. Iranian Shah wanted an alternative energy source since he considered Iranian natural oil reserves predetermined. Furthermore, Iran also regarded that the nuclear technology would raise Iranian regional and global stature by bringing it in the category of developed and technologically advanced nations of the world. However, in the later course of time, the general ambitions clearly indicated that Iran remained pragmatic and could seek for the nuclear weapon if so needed, which suggest that Iran would take any step to if its national interests is at stake and the option of the nuclear weapon cannot be ruled out. Although Iran sign the Nuclear Non-Proliferation Treaty. Iran has never officially admitted the making of nuclear bomb just like North Korea. Iranian government was constantly in touch with the international community till the final settlement of its nuclear issue with the P5+1 powers. Iran adopted a strong stand in every diplomatic forum about its nuclear programme , the official of Iran are denying any development of nuclear technology for making weapons. (Hassani 2016)

Iranian stances towards nuclear arms is inspired from various factors including its view of the world, its conceived role in the global politics, its core values and interest including religious expansionism, and various lessons which it derived from recent history with the occasions of the US invasion of Afghanistan and Iraq. Moreover, the Iran's ambitions to expand its military power to challenge the regional balance of power addressed the goals of generally political nature as a response to particularly perceived threats from rival states. In the later course of time, the acquisition of nuclear technology could easily help Iran to reach a certain level of security when it was surrounded by many adversaries in the region. With such an option, the Iranian threat perception could outline the capability to expand its power and meet all the existential challenges. (Chan 2016).

Inherently, there are various plausible reasons and motivations for Iran's pursuit of withdrawing its nuclear program and reaching at a point of consensus with the international community. Despite every effort by Iran to acquire the nuclear weapons besides various implications Iran refrain to acquire such motives. Iran is bounded by the NPT, which prohibits development of the nuclear weapons and thus any breach towards this effect would draw intense international criticism and lead to a great deal of international pressure placed on it. The reason for efforts of acquisition of the nuclear weapons by Iran would change the Iranian calculations on the cost benefit analysis thus making it bolder and unpredictable which subsequently would result in multiple and complex problems and reduce the chances of deterring Iran from indulging in any brinkmanship kind of behavior. To understand the diplomacy and strategies of Iranian official, we should carefully and intently look at the moves and actions of actors on the basis of rational actor model. The Iranian official will go for the best available options regarding its nuclear porgramme because rational actor model suggest that human being are rational and opt best available option, but at the same time Iran will maintain ambiguity regarding its nuclear programme to gain maximum benefits from the international community. (Fiedler 2016) The failure of implementation of nuclear deal with the international community will lead Iran to opt for progress in its nuclear programme. Iran would like to keep working on the option of its nuclear programme for its future options. The nuclear programme will also help Iran in development of its ambition of regional hegmoney.

Furthermore, in such a scenario of probability, Iran after acquiring the nuclear capability would use it as means to change the rules of the game in the region. However, what lack to be highlighted is that the nuclear weapons have to be placed under the military command to make them effective or else they do not serve the purpose of deterrence. More so, the nuclear weapons have hardly proved to be a successful tool of coercion and lose their efficacy if used for any other purpose of deterrence. This argument about Iran attracts the international community that Iran is inflexible and can go to any limit for power maximization of gaining the role of regional hegemony. The nuclear bomb is a tool for achieving its target. The situation in terms of the regional security will drastically change after the failure of nuclear deal particularly Iran having no more cooperative role with the international community. Following the situation in Iraq after the drawn down of the US forces and any possibility of pro-Iranian militias establishing their stronghold over southern Iraq will leave less chances for the world to counter the growing military capabilities of the Iran.

The fears if pro-Iranian militias successfully establish its hold over southern Iraq, no regional or extra-regional power will be able to challenge Iran in terms of military capability. It is also apprehensive that the current regime in Tehran, would get embolden and more openly and actively support militant organizations like Hezbollah and Hamas and those which are actively engaged in anti-state activities in states like Bahrain, Iraq and Yemen. Moreover, Iran, in usual assessment, has an expansionist ideological influence that will help in successfully establishing an alliance of many groups or states that are Shiite dominated or at least pro-Iran. Failure to the deal with P5+1 states, such a scenario would obviously alter the strategic balance of power in the region, and could also inspire the Shiite revolutionary Islamist movements, to seize the power from Sunni led monarchies in the Shiite dominated states of the Gulf and the Middle East. (Berti and Guzansky 2014)

The failure of American foreign policy in Iran led to the existing hostility between the two nations. He draws a comparison, between the US-Iran relations, which existed during the Shah's era and after the revolution and how the whole scenario affects the present day US-Iran equation. Overall, the book presents an excellent analysis of Iranian-American relations. There are certain levels of the difficulties that the United States and Iran face domestically in dealing with each other. The diplomatic crisis between Iran and the international community, especially the US and Europe can be traced back to the times of Iranian revolution, but the crisis over the nuclear diplomacy, actually started in 2002 after the details of Iran's clandestine uranium enrichment and plutonium production facilities became public. (Ansari 2006)

The consequences of a nuclear armed Iran with a scenario of catastrophic regional war will have dire consequences rather than placing Iran on a sound stage. The Nuclear weapon would have rather a negligible impact on the overall balance of military power in the Middle East. This assertion is based on the assumption, that Iran like any other nation is primarily concerned about its own security rather to establish hegemony on the region. Such conclusions are drawn by the author from the realist perspective which postulates that states in an international society would mainly be concerned in deterring other states, pursuing their quest for autonomy, and endeavoring for greater regional influence. Hossein ridicules the claims that if Iran, acquires the nuclear weapons it would or could deliver these to Hezbollah or Hamas to wage a proxy war against Israel. In his opinion neither the nuclear weapons could help in waging a proxy war nor could these be used for further proliferation to arm the Shiite states as in realist paradigm, all states are potential competitors and thus the likelihood of nuclear proliferation doesn't qualify. The ignorance of such historical fact about proliferation involving numerous reasons has exceptionally proliferated to other states. Like France, UK and US helped Israel in its nuclear program and similarly, the alleged A.Q Khan network supported enrichment of uranium and centrifuges to Iran that thus challenges the general claim. However, the logic of presenting Iran as a victim of aggression rather than hegemony, especially in the context of CIA led coup, Iran – Iraq war and the Israeli-US threats of attacking Iran, draw a diverse approach. Therefore, the Iranian behavior as reactionary in the overall complex regional matrix rather than offensive or threatening, of course to which most Western perception would also disagree. This notion rejects the assertion that Iran is sort of an existential threat to the state of Israel, which is used mostly by Israel as rhetoric to achieve sympathies of the western states despite its brutal treatment of the innocent Palestinians. (Mousavian 2012)

The US-Iran confrontation is not just about the nuclear program but rather is a much complex phenomenon that has its roots in the Iran's Islamic Revolution of 1979. This gulf was further widened once the US provided Iraq with chemical weapons consequently Iraq successfully used against Iran. Therefore, the confrontation is deeper and much intense than actually what it appears in the diplomatic circles. To unravel the myths from that of realities which keeps the relationship at the lowest ebb and also identifies factors which aggravates the tensions. Since 9/11, the relationship has taken a new turn. After the invasion of Afghanistan followed by Iraq, Iran viewed that it could be the next in line especially amid the "axis of evil" speech. Therefore, the author fears that the winning of election by President Muhammad Ahmadinejad the Iran-US confrontation may lead to a war in the region. Although scholars disagree about the best method by the United States to deal and ultimately restore its diplomatic relations with Iran, but after the election of Hassan Rouhani, most see an increasingly moderate stance by the newly elected Iranian government.

Following the nuclear deal with P5+1 powers, Iran as a rational actor like of any other state that is pursuing policies in line with its perceived national objectives and goals. The issues and implication with regards to the US policy towards Iran and argue that the United States' goals in Iran should be based on drawing the country away from the path of belligerent behavior by offering incentives and opportunities for trade and cooperation. In such way, the US policy towards Iran experience shortsightedness and has only helped the hardliners to gain popularity by selling anti-American sentiments even after economic stagnation which they have effectively attributed as a consequence of "victimization" by the US. Therefore, the policy makers at the Capitol Hill need to formulate a more balanced approach that caters for both positive incentives, if Iran changes its behavior, as well as punitive measures in case of non-compliance. The researchers further explore the common areas of interest between the two states in various fields which could be jointly pursued after introducing confidence building measures into the equation. (Elasrag, 2015)

Despite the apparent deal between Iran and P5+1 power, the Arab league is much concerned about Iran's nuclear threat. Iranian top leadership has repeatedly ruled out any possibility of intent of developing any nuclear bomb. They maintain the claim that their nuclear program is for peaceful purpose. The issue of Iran nuclear weapon is more complicated due to the stance of Saudi Arabia regarding Iran nuclear programme. The efforts of Saudi Arabia and Iran for the joint peaceful settlement of issues can lead to the peace and security in the region because the arms race and desire for regional hegemony is one of the main factor for insecurity in the region. The poor diplomatic relations and sectarian division between both countries is adding fuel to the rivalry and competitive behavior towards each other. The tension between both countries has also divide the other regional actors due to their feeling of insecurity. There is no possibility of using hard power or stance by other states regarding any one of them, due to their own constrains.

Iran's proclamation for its military power is not aimed at harming Muslim countries but to make region strong through a certain level of balance of power. Therefore, Iran, which has achieved success in nuclear technology, should convince the Gulf regional states about the peaceful nature of its nuclear program and that the cooperation between Iran and the Arab states would help to improve the critical condition of the region.

In international approach with regards to responses to Iranian nuclearization are more aggressive in nature to deal with Iran for core regional issues. It rather needs to attempt to have a sort of broader dialogue between all the stakeholders. It is widely discussed that to attain strategic deterrence, the government of United States should adopt the policy of denial combine with jeopardy. There should be some forces to meet the challenge of growing military expansion and proxies of Iran in the Middle Eastern region if needed. The policy of Jeopardy can be utilized to hit two important sector of Iran, which are the strength of Iranian influence in the region, one is the military strength of Iran and second is oil which is the most valuable asset of Iran. The policy of denial and jeopardy are the two best options which are currently available to the United States of America for influencing the decision of Iranian regime in case of non compliance.

Mostly it has been observed that the Iranian leadership approach towards the nuclear issues and weapon of mass destruction is based on realistic approach instead of theoretical. There is need of understanding the political and military aspects of post revolution period rather than generalization of issues related with Iran nuclear ambitions and regional influence.

Thus, Tehran constantly struggles to dissuade all the extra-regional players out of the Middle East. Iranian nuclear deal is significant point of political gains, because Iran is located in a volatile region of Middle East where Israel, a close ally of the United States is already having a nuclear weapons capability.

US-IRAN NUCLEAR DEAL: POWER DYNAMICS FOR IRAN AND SAUDI ARABIA

The Western pressure, especially of the US, against Iran is not only due to its nuclear activities, but Iran's Middle East policies stand inconsistency with United States. The Iranian support for proxies like Hizbullah and Hammas, both of which have violent behavior towards Israel, and support of opposition forces in the different parts. These are main some of the significant causes of concern against Iran from the regional states.

are causes of strong concern for Iran, which indicate the thorough Iran-US contradictions. The previous course of actions reiterated that the militarization is not in favor of the regional state. This emphasizes on the need of cooperation between Gulf countries and Iran to struggle towards a common goal of ensuring peace and stability in the region through a variety of available options of cooperation rather than indulging into the quandaries. The existence of cooperating neighbors in the Middle Eastern region is not only a reason for progression but also shuns the concerns of prolong conflicts otherwise, it can also disturb the equation of power leading to weak economies and exceedingly putting finances in the procurement of armaments to undermine threats emanating from the hostile sides. (Menashri 2014)

In this regard, it is pertinent to establish confidence-building measures in the Gulf region by withdrawing nuclear programs and utilizing effective tools to fade down the ambitions of undermining each other through military power. These CBMs will enhance the security and peace in the Middle Eastern region, which will also reduced the role of foreign power in the region especially great power for their vested interests in the region.

It significantly offers a broad range of prospective cooperation that is imperative to understand why peace in the general interest of the regional states is inevitable. This helps in understanding the motivations and inspirations of regional states to have an insight into the nature of cooperative relationship with Iran and to shun the existing mistrust between other states in Iran's and its neighboring states.

With respect to Iran's relations with Western countries, it is generally speculated that Iran will eventually challenge the international status-quo following its political and economic autonomy in the result of a successful nuclear deal with the international community. The Iranian ambition would just focus on achieving that capability to remains just at the top and improve its bargaining position in the international politics. For instance, if It appears that Iran has mustered enough technology to be able to acquire nuclear technology but still waiting to strengthen its political and economic position and resume the nuclear ambitions in coming future. Such stances to add military dimensions to the Iranian nuclear issues could subsequently be divert the anticipated goals of nuclear deal with Iran and leave less in hand to peacefully end the lasting controversies through enduring blame games.

The USA and western countries buy minimum ten to fifteen years of time for rollback the existing nuclear programme of Iran. Iran cheats on the terms and conditions of JCPOA and monitoring and watch agencies, it would lead to serious violation of internationally accepted agreement by five permanent powers of Security Council and Germany. There is difference of opinion amongst analyst about JCPOA due to the gradual and step by step roll back of existing facilities of Iran nuclear installation. There are two types of views about this deal; some view this deal waste of time and deception by Iranian authority for political and economic gain while some are of the opinion that this deal will bring some radical changes in the policies of Iran toward serious concerns raised by the western world.

US-IRAN NUCLEAR DEAL: POWER DYNAMICS FOR IRAN AND SAUDI ARABIA

The opponent and supporter of Iran nuclear deal differ in opinion regarding its implication on the regional security and peace. Unarmed Iran without nuclear bomb will ensure the security not only for Arab states but also for the Israel, it will overall improve situation in the Middle Eastern region. Moreover, the better regional security situation will lead to more integration of the Middle Eastern states with each other and western world. The integration of regional and extra regional countries will improve the economic and political situation of the country. There are some point of cohesion between Iran and west especially regarding fighting against non-state actors like ISIS and dismantling other militant group in the region to secure not only the Middle Easter region but also Europe and rest of the world. Critics of Iran nuclear deal argues that allowing Iran civil nuclear activities will provoke the other regional states into the competition for acquiring the nuclear weapons / technology. They are also of the opinion that the unfreezing funds or Iran will also lead to aggressive behavior toward region and will sponsored proxies with the released amount.

Theoretical Aspect of Nuclear Deal

The balance of power in any region depends on great powers and super power(s) involvement and the ways in which such powers are engaged in regional systems. The great powers are in a better position to affect regional balances because of their superior capabilities and the local actors' dependence on them. The US involvement in the Middle Eastern region can be assessed in this context. States attempt to prevent a potential hegemony of one state by balancing against it. It is either through internal balancing or external balancing, where in internal efforts such as moving to increase economic capability, developing good strategies, increasing military power. In external balancing, states take external measures to counter the power of the opponent. The United States and conservative Arab regimes of the Middle East region believe that the Islamic The world should concentrate on the issue of Iran, which is one of the rough states in the region, posing threats to the other regional rivals including the US's Allies. The policy of deterrence should be the best policy, which can be adopted by great powers headed by the United States to prevent any possible threat pose by Iran. According to the concept of axis of evil given by the United States which is propagated by different countries mostly rival of Iran for the purpose to cut off Iran diplomatic relations with international community.

Iran is making this nuclear deal as external arrangements to counter Saudi Arabian influence in the region. According to neorealist the nature of international system is anarchic due to the ordering principle and distribution of capabilities and number of great powers in the international system. There is no central authority, and every state is treated as an equal entity in international system. Every state is sovereign and equal in the international system which follows its interests and work for attaining maximum security through self-help. The prime interests of a state s are to ensure their survival through any mean. This notion is not merely confined to the issues of morality or sacrifice of the national interest on the expense of friendly states. The change is always prevalent and the success of any state in the international arena of any state depends on maximization of their chances of survival and pursuance of national interests. This covers all the areas of national interest whether they may be termed as economic, political, security and even the cultural interest and the survival of the nation-state. This phenomenon sometimes creates a sense of competition, mistrust and uncertainty amongst sovereign states that ultimately leads towards the security dilemmas. The states in such a situation face serious confusions when two friendly states run across cut-throat competition.

US-IRAN NUCLEAR DEAL: POWER DYNAMICS FOR IRAN AND SAUDI ARABIA

Every sovereign State needs capabilities to achieve its security. The fear of relative gain reduced the chances of cooperation amongst states in the international anarchic system. The desire for maximum relative power by states leads to balance of power and create security dilemma which is face by all the states. There are two types of balancing by state which are internal balancing of power and external balancing of power. The states grow their capabilities through economic or military growth while in external balancing state enters in to the alliances to counter the power of other states.

As this deal concerns and involves different regional and international actors, after the deal IAEA (International Atomic Energy Agency) inspection team can monitor the nuclear program of Iran and limit the arms race in the region. It can enhance the insecurity in the Middle East and distrust between the regional states especially Saudi Arabia and Iran that also show their intention in acquiring nuclear technology. (E.G. Tan, 2016) Iran is of the view that it has got a due right to have a peaceful nuclear program to meet its growing demand of energy in the coming future. World community imposed sanctions on Iran due to the suspicious nuclear program of Iran's tilt and support toward non-state actors in the region. This suspicious clandestine Iran's nuclear program led to serious distrust between Iran and the international community.

All the rival states in the region try to impose the policies of their own national interests and therefore indulge in the arms race. Iran and Saudi Arabia are trying to attain the maximum level of security for itself, which is causing insecurity for the other actor. Both countries are attempting to increase their role and influence directly and indirectly through different means in the region. These means include direct military buildup, insurgent proxies, economic incentives, political influence, and religious and sectarian means. The US-Iran nuclear deal, which has far reaching political, economic and security consequences for the region. With regard to security repercussions, the nuclear agreement has cooled down the fiery declarations made by different regional actors including Saudi Arabia, Israel, and Turkey. The Israel's government directly threats (to attack Iran's nuclear facilities or installations) if Iran succeeded in acquiring the nuclear weapons. However, the results and consequences which emerge after the US-Iran nuclear deal are very strategic and vital not only for Saudi Arabia and other regional actors as well due to its impact on the existing regional balance of power between Saudi Arabia and Iran.

2 INTERNATIONAL EFFORTS TOWARDS NUCLEAR DEAL

Background of Iran Nuclear Program

Historically, the imaginative plans of Iranian King Reza Shah to were to built 20 nuclear plant in thirty years, which would help in meeting the energy demand of Iran. The then head of state Reza Shah focused on the nuclear programme which will achieved the target of 23 thousands megawatts of electricity. In the year 1977, Iran established Atomic Energy Organization of Iran (AEOI) and allocated a huge budget allocated for its operations. Iran spent a lot of money on the Research and development of nuclear programme. This progamme was started with great enthusiasm and zeal keeping in view the future needs and demand of the country.

Shortly in the aftermath of the training of nuclear scientists, the second goal was setup for the search operation in hunt of uranium mines essentially prerequisite of acquiring the nuclear technology. Moreover, to meet the demands of uranium within Iran and some other external option also explored for attainment of sufficient level of uranium reserves.

However, with the advent of the Islamic revolution of Iran and the hostility between the US and Iran due to the hostage of the US diplomatic mission in Tehran, the United States came up with rigid foreign policy towards Iran. The three decade era of bitter relationship between Iran and the US has greatly affected the diplomatic and economic strength of Iran. Shah of Iran had pour a huge amount of its budget to the nuclear programme of Iran. In the catastrophic war between Iran and Iraq, Iran explored different options for restarting its nuclear programme with help of foreign assistant. But this time the international community especially United States and Israel were not in good diplomatic and political term with Iran, which was causing hurdles for Iran to continue its nuclear programme with the same pace. The possible threat from great power after revolution towards Iran led the government to consider the option of the nuclear weapon for its survival and security in the region. It was unacceptable for Israel to have nuclear armed Iran in Middle eastern region. Israel was considering different options to neutralize the Iranian nuclear program including air strikes on the different sites of nuclear installation or facility inside Iran. Apparently Iran nuclear programme during the era of Shah was for civilian purpose but after the revolution it was not for peaceful purpose, although the government of Iran denied any intention of nuclear bomb. The government of Iran had signed the NPT agreements and later on ratified it in 1970. (Flanagan & Wall, n.d.)

However, the upcoming era of nuclear cooperation between Iran and other European states like France, Sweden, Germany and also the US itself completely changes the landscape of the controversial nuclear program. (Kahl, Dalton, & Irvine, 2012) The current Iranian President Hassan Rouhani shortly weeks after coming into power, Iran followed a hardliner stance on its objectives of acquiring nuclear technology for the energy purposes and stood under the limelight on the stage of global politics since it was accused by the US and other countries for diverting the civilian technology for the military purposes. Present view of the Iran, which is now changed and maintain that it's legal for Iran to pursue its peaceful nuclear programme to meet its future energy demand. Iranian President criticized the west for having double standards regarding nuclear proliferation in the region. The nuclear activities were restarted in 2006 after accusing the international community for dishonoring their words by failing to provide fuel from outside as per agreement. He also blame that more sanctions were imposed on Iran to further damage the economy of Iran. After refusal of signing the additional protocols, the international community including Arab states blamed Iran for secretly developing its nuclear programme for making the nuclear weapons and posing a threat to regional and international peace. According to the Director National Intelligence (DNI), in one of his estimate that it is very difficult to identify the exact intention of Iran but if Iran continue with the same pace of progress and it wants to build a weapon, then it will take further at least ten more years to develop any nuclear device.

Later on, the negotiations on Iran's nuclear issue constricted in extent at the very initially stage, since those mainly focused on dissuading Iran from acquiring the nuclear weapons and in return the sanctions may ease. However, the international effort to prevent Iran from the possibility of acquiring the nuclear weapons through the deal has several unfold implications for the rest of the region. The historical enmity between Iran and the Arab world is particularly influence on the grounds of promotion of particular religious ideology by either side respectively. In addition, the regional security milieu is under several conflicts including Yemen, Syria and other parts of the Middle East however; the nuclear deal also enhances the chances of Iran's political, economic and the security role and influence across the region. The growing influence of Iran definitely causes severe unease in the Arab world.

The Global Consensus on Nuclear Non-Proliferations

The global experiences of nuclear destruction in the aftermath of the nuclear attacks on Hiroshima and Nagasaki in 1945, the international community collectively has been striving to overcome such an incident in future. However, yet many states carried out their efforts for getting nuclear technology either for civilian or military purposes. The Atom for Peace proposal of the US President Eisenhower in 1953 was the program to promote the nuclear technology for peaceful purposes moreover in 1957 the same resulted in establishment of an international organization under the United Nations. Initially, the traces of Iranian nuclear program also portray it as primarily a brainchild of the initiative of the US President Dwight D. Eisenhower's program of Atom for Peace designed with particular objectives of extending nuclear technology to underdeveloped states under the program. (Cheney & Cheney, n.d.) The International Atomic Energy Agency (IAEA) setup with the main goals to promote the nuclear technology for civilian and peaceful purposes, similarly it was also given the mandated to control the proliferation of the nuclear technology for military purposes. Later on, in 1997, the Model Additional Protocol (INFCIRC/540) endorsed under the IAEA (International Atomic Energy Agency) board of governors in order to further improve the international efforts for the nuclear non-proliferation.

US-IRAN NUCLEAR DEAL: POWER DYNAMICS FOR IRAN AND SAUDI ARABIA

The Nuclear Non-Proliferation Treaty opened to sign in 1968 and entered into force in 1970, was an effort of curbing any further chances of the nuclear weapon acquisition and stooping the nuclear capable states from the using the nuclear weapons during wars. The NPT since its inception has been under severe criticism on the grounds that it only privileges and confers the status of *de-jure* status to those 'five nuclear powers' who acquired the nuclear weapons prior 1968 but leaves no room for others. Moreover, the NPT also prohibits and strongly dissuades states from acquiring the nuclear capability. Moreover, the states on the pretext of acquiring nuclear capability for the civilian and energy purposes is still another topic of debate. The non-nuclear states feel the nuclear capability merely guarantees their security and survival in the modern era of military technology. The expensive arms procurement for instance never lets developing countries to concentrate other sides such as economic and social development of their society. The costly arms race drags states to allocate a bulk of their economic resources for the security purposes whereas, the limited quantity of the nuclear weapons only costs them one time but in turn assures their security against any aggression and the breakout of warfare. (Einhorn, n.d.)

International Community response to Iran Nuclear Program

The world community responds in the shape of economic and diplomatic pressure to limit the Iranian nuclear capability for nuclear bomb. In 2003, Iran promises to cooperate with the international community and shows its commitment for suspension of Uranium enrichment. Iran sign additional protocol to NPT in December 2003 despite of opposition from Majlis. The EU-3 and Iran sign "Paris agreement" in November 2004 for starting trade and aid talks. The US governments welcome the agreement between EU-3 and Iran. The Iranian government rejects the proposal of peaceful use of nuclear technology with no security provision in 2005. On August 2005 Iran violate the IAEA (International Atomic Energy Agency) security measures and again start work on its nuclear program at Esfahan nuclear installation.

Nuclear proliferation is an international issue. There are few countries in the world i.e. USA, Russia, France, China, United Kingdom, North Korea, Israel, Pakistan and India, which have declared of having nuclear weapon systems but more than thirty states having capacity to quickly regain nuclear power including Germany, Japan, South Korea etc. The issue of nuclear proliferation is of great concern not only for the major nuclear powers but also for the non-nuclear powers. There is a global consensus on the issue of nuclear non-proliferation, which is for making the world more safer for the human beings. Further the United Nation Security Council resolution No. 1887 stresses for the need of disarmament of even the nuclear nations. The number of member states who ratified the CTBT increased to one hundred and fifty seven, (157) in December, 2011. There are some success stories of global non-proliferation regimes, which work very well in some cases but there are also some examples of failure in case of India, Israel, Pakistan and North Korea.

The US administration announced to join the EU-3 group to expand the groups and also include some other members. The group was renamed as P5+1 consist of Germany, US, China, Russia, UK and France. In June 2006 P5+1 offer incentive in case of compliance and sanction for not cooperating.

US-IRAN NUCLEAR DEAL: POWER DYNAMICS FOR IRAN AND SAUDI ARABIA

United Nation Response to Iran Nuclear Program

The United Nations Security Council (UNSC) adopted seven different resolutions to undertake firm international efforts to overcome the Iran's nuclear crisis. Particularly, the key demands asked Iran to cooperate with the international community through a serious of confidence building measures and immediately halt the uranium enrichment program. Approximately all the resolutions adopted in the light of Chapter VII of the UN Charter enforce Iran's adherence with the legally binding resolutions. Furthermore, four resolutions address the imposition of economic and business sanctions Iran as an effort to compel the Islamic Republic to refrain from acquiring the Weapons of Mass Destruction (WMDs). The P5+1 especially the USA admin formed a new strategy of negotiating to solve the issue of Iran nuclear program through peaceful means in February 2009. P5+1 resume dialogue with Iran after the issuance of proposal by Iranian September 2009. ("The U.N. Resolutions | The Iran Primer", 2016)

Israel's Stance on the US-Nuclear Deal

Prior to the Islamic revolution in Iran, Israel had cordial and close relations with the former since both states shared common interests in the geostrategic context. Moreover, Iran also considered Israel as a counterweighing regional power against the hostile Arab nations. It was their shared interest that both the states continued their interactions particularly amidst the oil-embargo by Arab States in 1973 however, Iran continued its export of the oil to Israel. (Norell, 2015). The amiable relationship soon shifted in the aftermath of the Islamic revolution in Iran and consequent support to Palestinian Liberation Organization and Shia and other militias like Hamas and Hezbollah in the surroundings of Israel. ("Nuclear done deal", 2015). The delicate security situation of the Muslim states in the immediate neighborhood of Israel encouraged Iran to establish small groups of Shia militias that in turn could provide it a strategic edge over regional competitor particularly against Arab countries and the Israel.

Israel has a perception of Iran as an emerging threat that sponsors the non-state Shia militias besides advancement in nuclear program. Particularly, the 2006 Israel-Hezbollah war further deteriorated the regional strategic situation since the threat of expanding power of militant groups under Iran's patronage developed a scenario of great security risk for Israel in its regional ambitions. The recurring threats amidst Iranian President Ahmadinejad assertions to eliminate the Zionist state out of global map and the prospective nuclear armed-Iran was significantly exploited by Israel to portray and propagate later as greatest risk to the world and for Israel. (Skancke & Friedman, 2010).

The bitter experience of threat exchange between Iran and Israel besides a huge trust deficit exceedingly results Israel's opposition for a nuclear deal with Iran. The possibilities of nuclear capable or nuclear deal with Iran are both unacceptable choices for Israel since in both cases Israel and the Arab countries in the region are the mostly affected. The nuclear capability of Iran would trigger a threat of nuclear weaponization of the Iran sponsored militias whereas in case of possible nuclear deal, Iran would enjoy greater economic prosperity in the course of subsequent lifting of economic sanction. (Herzog, 2015).

The Joint Comprehensive Plan of Action (JCPoA)

In 2009, Iran announced that it want to get fuel for the 5MW Tehran Research Reactor (TRR) which produces radioisotopes for medical purpose. The Iranian authorities also agreed to swap its 1200kg of low enriched uranium to place in Turkey, in return for nuclear fuel for the TRR.

Turkey and Brazil that subsequently led to signing the Tehran Declaration on May 17, 2010 between Turkey, Iran and Brazil welcomed the announcement. The deal however was rejected by the US and the internal politics of Iran became a hurdle. Some of the Iranian leaders wanted to attach further conditions with the swap deal and therefore, it could not make any further headway.

The deal however, did show some signs of flexibility in Iranian stance to which the Russians initiated their own diplomatic efforts to resolve the Iranian nuclear issue. In July 2011, Russian Foreign Minister Sergei Lavrov proposed a systematic road map during his visit to Washington. (Ben-Meir, 2009) At the initial stage of the proposal, Iran supposed to limit the enrichment activities at Natanz reactor and stop further installation of centrifuges. In return, the P 5+1 would ease some of the sanctions. As a next step, Iran would bring down the enrichment level to five and would allow IAEA (International Atomic Energy Agency) greater access to monitor and verify the activities and the UN along with the P 5+1 would lift most of the sanctions against Iran. In third step, Iran would implement the IAEA (International Atomic Energy Agency) additional protocol in return for all the UN and P 5+1 sanction to be suspended temporarily. Finally, Iran would have to suspend all the enrichment related activities and the international community would lift all the sanctions imposed on Iran. Although the initial American reaction was negative but the negotiations continued for implementation on the systematic proposed formula. Iran also offered its own proposal while P 5+1 gave their own conditions which were first discussed in May 2012 in Baghdad and next in Moscow in June 2012. (Schneider, 2013)

Notably, the talks did not yield any conclusive results, however the negotiations continued for almost whole of the year. The next critical round of negotiations between Iran and the P 5+1 were held in Almaty in April 2013 but both the sides remained dissatisfied with each other and thus no final agreement could be concluded. The negotiations again started in November 2013 in Geneva and the change in the Iranian government finally did finally bring some good news for the world.

The new Iranian negotiator Javad Zarif and the new pragmatic Iranian leader Hassan Rouhani were the key players from the Iranian side while on the US side it was flexibility shown by President Obama despite Israeli and hardliner's pressure who made this interim deal or Joint Action Plan possible. For the reason that of the deal Iran would be able to carry out some limited economic activities with its European partners in gold, pharmaceuticals and automobiles besides gaining access to 4.2 million dollars that earlier frozen due to sanctions. (Tarock, 2016)

It was stated by President Barrack Obama in 5th August 2015 speech at an American university, "Despite the criticism we moved ahead to negotiated a more lasting comprehensive deal". He further stated that his Secretary of State John Kerry worked with allies and achieved this deal through diplomatic means. He also appreciated the role of Secretary of Energy Ernie Moniz, who worked on all the technical information. He termed this deal as historical and comprehensive which will meet all the needs and requirements of the international community regarding the peaceful and acceptable management of Iranian nuclear program. Despite Obama's Administration successful deal he faced severe criticism from the international community and within the country but it firmly reached a mutually agreeable solution to the Iran's nuclear issue, which shows that this deal is the result of successful diplomacy on the side of the US administration to meet its objective and aims. (Secretary, 2015)

3 IRAN NUCLEAR DEAL AND ITS IMPACT ON MIDDLE EASTERN REGION

The issue of Iranian nuclear deal has significantly gained an important place on the stage of international politics. Throughout the course of controversial nuclear program, Iran had been showing a continuous resilience on its stance of uranium enrichment and mastering nuclear fuel cycle. Regardless of the Iranian nuclear intentions, the intensive diplomacy and negotiations on the Iranian nuclear program has raised the stature of Iran in the region. Owing to historical Iran–Arab rivalry, the strategic arms race continued to prevail in the Middle East, primarily as a reason to Iranian uncompromising behavior on the nuclear issues. Despite the efforts for resolution of alleged Iranian nuclear weapons program, the agreement between Iran and the global negotiators on the nuclear issue, the conventional arms race in the region never stopped since some of the regional states might consider having a nuclear option of their own. This could trigger other state in troubled regions like East Asia or even Europe to evaluate the nuclear option with the dwindling the US military power. (Kahl, Dalton, & Irvine, 2012)

The tension between Iran and the international community has been a significant issue of discussion. Right from its beginning the nuclear deal with Iran has been severely criticized on the grounds that it will further jeopardize the existing status-quo of regional security milieu. Particularly it will create a considerable brazen out situation to the security in the Middle Eastern region and the beyond due to Iran's geostrategic position and its response on different issues.

Iran and the Middle East

The recent agreement on the nuclear programme between Iran and western power raised a hope for peace and stability in the Middle Eastern region. It is fact that this agreement will not addressed all of the outstanding issues of Iran with West or Arab countries including Israel, but it will reduced the tension between Iran and Middle Eastern countries, due to enhanced security arrangements. Although the US invasion of Iraq did not significantly changed the political and geostrategic map of Middle Easter but it played a very important role in strengthening the influence of Iran in the region. The instability of Middle East is contributing to the stronger role of Iran with the help of proxies, but it is insufficient to challenge the hegemony of United States in the region. Another phenomena of Arab spring is also one of the contributing factor in dominance of Shiite groups because in many areas of Arab countries, Shiite are in majority under dictatorial Sunny minority. Still, these Shiite populations can influence the central authority or governments. Iran is supporting the Shiite groups in different part of the Middle East in the same fashion as of Moscow support for communist groups in third world countries. The resumption of Russian relations with different countries in the region is also in the favor of Iran, because Iran and Russia are enjoying good relations with each other since a long time. There are some common interests of Russia and Iran in the region and both have a common strong competitor in shape of the USA.

The consequences of the failure of interim nuclear agreement between Iran and P5+1 powers, the Arab world will view a nuclear-armed Iran ruled by a hardliner regime as an existential threat. In addition to that, same concern is also shared by the Israel since it is a very small state and even a small nuclear device detonated on Israeli territory could make it uninhabitable for the generations to come and would practically make it extinct. Israel has a history of preempting perceived nuclear dangers in past and the case of attack over Iraqi nuclear reactor at Osirak in 1982, a Syrian suspected nuclear facility in 2007 and Sudanese weapon factory in 2012 are just few cases in point. Israeli military have made elaborate plans for such an eventuality where if the government takes a political decision on striking Iran, they should have already plans made up for execution. Numerous times such rehearsals have taken place and the belief amongst some of the senior military commanders are confident that such a strike after due deliberation can be successfully executed. If such an attack goes ahead, it could result in Iranian retaliating back on Israeli targets that could subsequently involve other regional states and non-state actors as well thus spilling the conflict to a larger spectrum. This strategic competition and rivalry over nuclear and political issues could escalate into a full-scale regional war thus even involving states outside the region that apparently would become a highly destabilizing scenario. (Zak, 2016)

Nuclear Armed Iran and Regional Hegemony

The successful establishment of the pro-Iranian militia stronghold in the southern Iraq, there will be fewer chances for many states to challenge Iran in military terms. The current regime in Tehran, would get embolden and more openly and actively support militant organizations like

Hezbollah, Hamas, and those which are actively engaged in anti-state activities in states like Bahrain, Iraq and Yemen. Such a scenario would obviously alter the strategic balance of the region, and could inspire the Shiite revolutionary Islamist movements, to snatch the power from Sunni led monarchies in Shiite dominated states. (Lerner, 2008) The failure of American foreign policy in Iran would subsequently further fuel the hostility between the two nations. A comparison, between the US-Iran relations, which existed during the Shah's era and after the revolution and how the whole scenario affects the present day US-Iran equation.

One of the principal reasons for Iranian inflexibility on the nuclear issues is that Iran wants to show the world that it is one of the leading states in civilized nations. This demonstration in the Iranian perception can come through advancement and development in the fields of nuclear, defence and space technologies that thus could apparently enhance its prestige not only at the regional level but also in eyes of rest of the world. The Great Persian Empire, which once extended from River Indus to Mediterranean Sea dates back to 550 B.C. and Iranians are extremely conscious and aware of their historical legacy thus they take extreme pride in their ancient history. The Iranian youth and majority of the public also view Iranian nuclear program as symbol of development and national pride and thus regard it as a status symbol amongst the developed nations. The support for the Iranian nuclear program is widespread, not only due to the reason that the Iranian youth feels protected from any external invasion or aggression, but mainly because it gives them confidence that Iran is on its way to prosperity and making progress even in the most sophisticated fields of nuclear technology.

A nuclear Armed Iran could incite nuclear excitement in the region. Not only other states like Saudi Arabia, Egypt and many other countries of the

Arab world could also seek the options of developing and possessing the nuclear weapons but Israel could decide to bring its bomb out of the closet. The prevalent speculations about the Saudi intentions instigate the possibility of acquiring the nuclear weapons to counter the Iranian threat is another reason for concern in the region. The extent of exploring options could escalate to seek an external assistance to provide the Kingdom with the nuclear weapons in case of rising tensions. Therefore, the Iranian nuclear bomb could motivate other regional states to seek for their own nuclear weapons. Such factors, in turn affect the nuclear decision making process amongst states located in volatile regions like South Korea and Japan besides, the regional states like Egypt, Saudi Arabia, Jordan and even UAE. Such a scenario could possibly result in making the nuclear domino theory a self-fulfilling prophecy. For instance, the North Korean withdrawal from the NPT and its subsequently testing of the nuclear weapon had casted a negative shadow on the global efforts directed towards nuclear disarmament. North Korea has seen a precedent that any state that possesses the nuclear weapons can even risk defiance in front of a global imperial power while others like Libya and Iraq lacking deterrent cannot save themselves from decimation even through compliance and appeasement(Tzeng, 2015). The aim of achieving a nuclear free zone in Middle East would thus become a least probability that would make the dream about abolishment of the nuclear weapons from face of the planet as redundant and unachievable. (Hitchcock, 2016)

Another view behind the Iranian nuclear program follows the traces by inciting deliberate controversies in the program, Iranian policy makers want to gain a higher strategic bargaining position, which could also help them in achieving some of their regional objectives. The rationale behind this assumption dictates that Iran wants a regional stature but the rich energy resources in Middle East and the interests of great powers like the US, Russia and China undermines the perceived Iranian regional pre-eminence. Consequently, the Iranian leadership seeks to use the nuclear program and the controversies thereon to create tense environments where the Western states are compelled to offer something tangible in return for the Iranian compliance with the IAEA (International Atomic Energy Agency) on its nuclear program ("The Leading rogue state: the United States and human rights", 2009) Therefore, the maximum chances of national interest held at high esteems since the desired tangible economic and political benefits in return for compliance with the negotiated deal otherwise the pursuance of nuclear option is always open choice for Iran.

The recent developments in the region lead to expansion of Iranian influence particularly after lifting of economic sanctions as a part of Joint Comprehensive Plan of Action (JCPOA) in January, 2016. The provisions of Joint Comprehensive Plan of Action (JCPOA) is definitely working toward the path of nonnuclear Iranian state but dismantling the capabilities of non-state actors and its support for proxies is still a question mark on the Iranian side. According to Capt retired Sean R. Liedman, United State Navy "It's all about the money" Stated another way, from money all power flows. Money is the lifeblood of Iran's support to its proxy groups, and the lifting of economic sanctions will provide Iran with more money to further achieve its objectives in the region". (Liedman, Opinion: Iran Nuke Deal Will Spawn More Proxy Attacks Like The Ones In Yemen, 2016)

Iran's Quest for Nuclear Program

To understand the role and state's motivation for acquiring the nuclear weapons includes the nuclear optimist argument that whether the nuclear weapons have contributed towards the global stability or is actually a recipe for a disaster waiting just for a right opportune, which may befall anytime in an anarchic world order. The states' desire to acquire the nuclear weapons has increased but very few have the capability to develop weapons because they are difficult to develop and maintain, therefore, only a handful of countries would like these to be possessed which creates a balancing order as these serves as an extremely useful mechanism of deterring the war. This situational distribution of power in the international system dictates state's behavior. Therefore, the more power a state acquires the more violent behavior it would adopt, which consequently balances the structure or equation. Although the nuclear weapons merely meant for deterrence, but there is no guarantee that these could or would never be used. States sometimes resort to behavior which can neither be termed rational nor proportionate to some given circumstances and thus could lead to situation which might involve use of the nuclear weapons. (Fiedler, 2016) There are certain organizational structures and mechanisms, which have their own interests, standard operating procedures, and customs which sometimes could remain outside the control of the political leadership, and therefore an accidental or an unauthorized use of the nuclear weapons would always remain a possibility. The political horizon has been playing a direct bearing or linkage with the Iranian nuclear program. The attack of chemical weapon on Iran by Saddam Hussain regime in 1983, which were provided by the USA at that time, was one of the major factors for reorganizing Iran nuclear programme. This attack changes the whole perceptions of Iranians regarding their security and the nuclear weapons. It also changes the threat perceptions of Iranians, which made them, realize that such attacks could possibly pose serious threats to its basic survival of Iranian people in the future. (Mannully, 2009) Iran put the matter of using chemical weapon against Saddam Hussain in the United Nation for condemning this act by Iraq, but the USA resisted and save the face of Iraq and Saddam Hussain from defamation in United Nations. All of this made Iranians realized that Iran has to take its own security measures in international anarchic system for its survival and security and the major powers were there only for their own vested interests.

The Israel factor is another issue of concern for the Iranian nuclear program since from very beginning, the Iranian Revolution regarded Israel as a foremost threat to its national security after the US. Despite maintaining an ambiguous posture over its nuclear program, the world clearly knows that Israel possesses the nuclear weapons. Israeli nuclear capability remains the driving force behind the Iranian desire to pursue the quest for developing the nuclear weapons. (Thakur, 2012)

Iranian nuclear program nourished with the blessing of Eisenhower's administration five decades, old program initiated for peaceful spread of nuclear technology under the Atoms for Peace program. Iranian Shah wanted an alternative energy source since he regarded its natural oil reserves are finite. Furthermore, Iran also regarded that the nuclear technology would raise Iranian regional and global stature by bringing it in the category of developed and technologically advance nation. Historically Iran followed a policy of developing nuclear arsenal even during the peacetime but it was an uneasy job for the reason that it was bound with the obligations of the treaty unlike the North Korea. Iran is signatory to the Nuclear Non-Proliferation Treaty and has been bound with the obligations of the treaty unlike the North Korea. Iran also wants to stay engaged with the international community and avoid isolation therefore; it has remained continuously engaged in negotiations with the western powers and has never closed its doors on them. (Kittrie, n.d.)

Therefore, the Iranian claims concerning its nuclear program remains hidden under the cloak of rhetoric and reality. Notably, the Iran's nuclear program since the Islamic Revolution of 1978 would be extremely helpful in understanding the priorities and nature of Iranian regime. Most of the authors are of the views that Iranian regional and extra-regional perspectives through the eyes of western prism that necessarily does not always give an accurate picture. It is highly essential to explore the state's behavior that could become the driving motive or intent for acquiring the nuclear weapons in his famous work. (Doyle, n.d.)

In addition, the Iranian stance towards nuclear arms is inspired from various factors, which support its stance on the grounds of recent invasions in Afghanistan and Iraq , and mainly because of the reasons that both states were unable to counter and dissuade the aggressor or at least properly handle the mere threats of invasion, while minimizing the risks. while minimizing the security risks and threats of aggression from the regional and outer-regional powers. The external threats to Iranian security perceptions to outlined the possible motivations behind Iran's quest for the nuclear weapons. Moreover, the various plausible reasons and motivations for Iran's pursuit of the nuclear weapons besides a variety of implications after Iran acquire this capability. The failure of agreement with the international community to resolve the enduring nuclear crisis, Iranian would opt for the progress of its nuclear program and ensure its dominant role in the regional affairs at any cost. Iran after acquiring the nuclear capability would use it as means to change the rules of the game in the region. More so, the nuclear weapons have hardly proved to be a successful tool of coercion and lose their efficacy if used for any other purpose of deterrence. Iran is adamant to use all means available at its disposal to dictate other of its status of a regional power, and the nuclear weapons option merely aims at achieving such objectives. (Yazdizadeh, Majdzadeh, Alami, & Amrolalaei, 2014)

The consequences of a nuclear armed Iran's which posits that nuclear such a scenario would not actually result in catastrophic regional consequences but rather would have a negligible impact on the overall balance of military power in the Middle East. This assertion based on the assumption, that Iran like any other nation is primarily concerned about its own security rather to establish hegemony on the region. The other perspective postulates that states in an international society would mainly be concerned in deterring other states, pursuing their quest for autonomy, and endeavoring for greater regional influence. The issue of Iran's nuclear weapons acquisition is alarming for many states that believe that after acquires the nuclear weapons it would deliver these to Hezbollah or Hamas to wage a proxy war against Israel. However, the Iranian behavior as been kind of mix of reactions in the overall complex regional matrix rather than offensive or threatening, of course to which most western scholars would disagree. The assertion that Iran is sort of an existential threat to the state of Israel believed as rhetoric to gain sympathies of the Western world.

The US-Iran confrontation is not just about the nuclear program but rather is a much complex phenomenon that has its roots in the revolution of 1979. This gulf was further widened once the US provided Iraq with chemical weapons that Iraq successfully used against Iran. Therefore, the confrontation is deeper and much intense than actually what it appears in the diplomatic circles. The realities of US-Iran relationship at the lowest ebb also identify certain factors, which aggravates the tensions and particularly in the post 9/11 era, the relationship has taken a new turn. After the invasion of Afghanistan followed by Iraq, Iran viewed that it could be the next in line especially amid the "axis of evil" speech. Therefore, then

President Muhammad Ahmedinejad proclaimed that the Iran-US confrontation may lead to a war in the region. However, in the prevailing context, the best method by the United States to deal and ultimately restore its diplomatic relations with Iran, but after the election of Hassan Rouhani, most see an increasingly moderate stance by the newly elected Iranian government. (Kimberlee, 2012)

Iran as a rational actor like of any other state that is pursuing policies in line with its perceived national objectives and goals. (Kemp, 2001) The US policy towards Iran viewed as shortsighted that merely helped the hardliners to gain popularity by selling anti-American sentiments even after economic stagnation that they have effectively attributed because of victimization by the US. Therefore, the policy makers at the Capitol Hill need to formulate a more balanced approach that caters for both positive incentives, if Iran changes its behavior, as well as punitive measures in case of non-compliance. The common grounds for their respective national interests by the US and Iran in a variety of diverse fields through cooperation and confidence-building measures could exceptionally assist both sides to overcome the existing gaps for collective benefit. There are many common grounds in Afghanistan, Central Asian region around Caspian and also in the Middle East which could have a lot in common between the US and Iran in future.

Iran Nuclear Program as a Bargaining Tool

The Joint Comprehensive Plan of Action signed in July 2015 in Vienna between Iran and France, China, Germany, Russia, the United Kingdom, the United States and the European Union. The nuclear deal provided an opportunity for creating an environment of confidence-building measures for the normalization of relationship between Iran and the international community. Moreover, as envisaged the objective through this normalization process was an effort to ensure that the Iranian nuclear program is merely for civilian and peaceful purposes. (Stone, 2015). The P5+1 Group consisting great powers eagerly pursued the mutually agreeable framework for the enduring controversy over Iranian nuclear program. However, at initial stage, the deal with Iran came under serious criticism and opposition by the US Congress. Besides many others, the high concerns also erupted from the Israel and Arab world particularly the Saudi Arabia.

The Obama administration came with firm commitment and efforts to address all the concerning stakeholders since its own behest, it was considered a historical move to resolve the enduring controversy through a political option. The objective oriented policies were moves to prevent Iran from acquiring the nuclear weapons before it could cross the threshold of obtaining the point of no return. Iran's economic sufferings amidst its allegedly clandestine attempt to shift its nuclear program from civilian to military purposes isolated the country from the international community.

The era of global interdependence is encompassed both challenges and opportunities for the states since, the isolation merely thwart the states from economic benefits. For its own national interest for Iran to come out of three-decade long political aloofness and the economic setbacks was a compulsion to accord with the international community and reach any possible resolution. The close draw up of the successful negotiations started to bring remarkable economic prospects for Iran. The reward of the implementing the commitments by Iran was gradual lift of sanctions after decades of tense relations between Iran and the West. The response was high welcome by the Iranian society with exceptional hopes of prospective political achievements along with immense economic opportunities and the prosperity. (Cheney & Cheney, n.d.)

The effort in tangible sense was a realization of the unsuccessful attempts of using force in the case of Iran since the high cost in terms of men and resources in the Iraq and Afghan war compelled the US to seek a mid way and resolve the issue through peaceful process. The high expectation as foreseen through the agreement forcing Iran to act as a responsible state in the international community however, was unwelcomed by the Arab world. However, besides the question of rolling back its nuclear program, the international community also sought Iran's role in resolving crises in Syria, Iraq and Yemen. The political move for the Iran-P5+1 nuclear deal also prospectively limited Iran's capability to influence the regional political and security dynamics by halting its allegedly sponsorship of Hezbollah, Hamas and other active militant groups in the Middle East.

Notably, unlike others Hezbollah is unusually has remained under patron of the Iran since, it allocates a huge amount of finances ranging up to 200 million dollar in a year. Apart from the financial support, the Lebanese Shia militia is also supported in terms of supply of latest weaponry, missile system, intelligence sharing, training of men and the logistic shore up. In addition, in the recent years Iran's undeviating support in the regional conflicts has enabled it to effortlessly pierce with the domestic affairs of many states like Syria, Yemen, and Lebanon and so on. The outlook of geostrategic scenario in the coming future with the influx of Iranian financial support for many other such militant groups that in expert opinion to some extent create an anarchic situation since such militia and the militant groups supported by Iran would be having upper hand than the governments of those countries. Moreover, in the post Iran and P5+ Iran's imperative geostrategic location and the role in the regional affairs and the critical involvement in the regional issues besides the nuclear agreement between Iran and the P5+1 not only alleviate the concerns risk of nuclear proliferation but also present significant implications for the future order of the Middle East. Whereas in the geostrategic landscape, the United States is apparently drawing away from it tradition allies. The swift inclination of the Obama administration as a matter of the fact in the course of nuclear deal with Iran, the scenario depicts to bring major shift in the regional balance of power. (Implementation of the Iran nuclear deal, n.d.)

The immense richness in terms of natural resources (oil and natural gas) along with the demographic edge over the Arab world specially Saudi Arabia having highly educated population are the means to hover the Iran's growing role in the international politics that could ultimately result in insightful changes within the Iran's social structure and its stature beyond the region. However, at moment the top most priority of the Iran's policy making elite obviously demonstrates overcoming the prolong effects of country's isolation and the economic revival after the lifting of economic sanctions. The other perspective usually perceived by the rival powers of Iran like Saudi Arabia and the Israel are encompassed with a mix of threats, challenges and growing imbalance of power in the region. After bargaining on its nuclear program, Iran would become more financially viable, politically on sound tracks and military strong than ever before. The Saudi Arabia and Israel foresee more chaotic and destabilized region will growing influx of the proxy forces sponsored by Iran and equipped with latest weaponry and the huge amount of funds.

Key Features of US-Iran Nuclear Deal

The Joint Comprehensive Plan of action (JCPOA) of Iran-P5+1

nuclear deal is an upfront snip of political achievements. The Iran's acceptance of harsh agreement regarding its nuclear program is apparently an effort to bring the prolong sanction to end, which is the hurdle in the way of progress and development since long. Despite the fact that Iran's cooperation with the international community is a subject to incessant monitoring of its nuclear sites. The main features of the nuclear deal bound Iran to follow the limitations on its uranium enrichment capacity. This agreement proposed reduction of Uranium enrichment from 19,000 to 5,000. This nuclear agreement also suggests that Iran would not cross the 3.67% purity level of enriched uranium for its peaceful use. (Robert Einhorn, 2016)

According the deal, the centrifuges will be removed from Fordow underground enrichment plant for next 15 years. In addition to the reduction of uranium enrichment. Iran will be bound to not export or import any kind of enriched uranium. Consequently, this will automatically limit Iran's uranium enrichment capacity of research and development in the years ahead. (Stone, 2015) Similarly, the heavy water reactors of Iran at Arak area will be removed and further bring certain technical limitations for Iran in the production and reprocessing of plutonium as well. To ensure the transparency of all these international measure, the deliberate and frequent inspection teams from International Atomic Energy Agency (IAEA) would have surprise visits to the nuclear and other suspicious non-declared sites of Iran. This process will enable the international community to access for the frequent inspection of those sites besides the in person inspection of those Iranian officials involved in the nuclear activities particularly since he last decade. (Elasrag, n.d.)

The successful compliments of Iran with all these international affairs result in the reduction of nuclear risk in the region subsequently such measures in turn would guarantee the relief of economic sanctions and the prevention of oil embargo. All these collectively facilitate in Iran's active participation in the international financial activities besides along with a recognized role in the international political and economic affairs. The international community and the United Nation Security Council will surpass the six harshest imposed sanctions on Iran for its allegedly clandestine nuclear program. Furthermore, this does not allow Iran to swiftly seek for the procurement of military hardware and armaments for another period of next five years besides in the course of the transfer of missile technology will bind Iran to remain refrained of such activities for next eight years. (Iran nuclear deal oversight, n.d.)

The year 2005 proved to be exceptionally diplomatically active year since from January 2005 to August 2005, the EU-3 numerous proposals floated from both the sides to strike a deal on the Iranian nuclear issue. In January, Iran offered proposal promising not to pursue weapons of mass destruction program and subsequently including negotiations on issues like regional security especially focusing on Afghanistan and Iraq, an undertaking that Iranian nuclear sites would remain immune from strikes, economic and trade issues and easing of sanctions. (Zetter, 2015) The EU 3 added to the list that Iran must adhere to the clauses of the agreement and suspend the uranium enrichment activities. The Additional Protocol and should suspend all enrichment and reprocessing activities. The negotiations continued and in August 2005, the EU-3 offered a comprehensive proposal that offered the following:

- An assured supply of low enriched uranium for the Iranian light water reactors.

- A stock of nuclear fuel stored in another country other than Iran.

- Iranian undertaking that to stop all work on nuclear fuel cycle technologies (a condition that though could be reviewed after 10 years)

- A formal assurance that Iran would not withdraw from the NPT.

- Commitment to sign the Additional Protocol.

- An agreement to return the spent nuclear fuel to supplier states.

- In return, EU would recognize Iran as a long-term trade partner in oil and energy.

- The cooperation between Iran and EU would be enhanced on issues like security (like Iraq and Afghanistan), terrorism, and drug trafficking and regional cooperation. (Bowen, Moran, & Esfandiary, n.d.)

Iran however, rejected the proposal on the pretext that no such commitments made in past were upheld by the international community and that theses offers doesn't recognize the Iranian inherent right of enriching uranium up to 20 percent. Russia, in order to broker a deal offered its own proposal in October 2005 offered Iran to share the ownership of a uranium enrichment plant in Russia to make sure that nuclear fuel is supplied uninterrupted to Iran. However, after negotiating for few months, Iran rejected the proposal in March 2006. In June 2006, Russia, China and the US joined the EU-3 and the negotiating party thus became P5+1.

From July 2006 to April 2009, numerous proposals were forwarded from both the sides that subsequently rejected by the other side. These proposals didn't add anything new to the August 2005 proposal but just was twist and turn to already identified issues which included, suspension of uranium enrichment activities by Iran, ensuring continuous nuclear fuel supply for Iranian reactors, cooperation with IAEA (International Atomic Energy Agency) under NPT and Additional Protocol, terrorism, nuclear and regional security etc. However, due to an inflexible stand on both the sides, no breakthrough could be achieved. (Cohen, 2010)

The other states like Turkey and Brazil also negotiated on the issues adding their own proposals but either side would ultimately reject some clause thereby not making it possible to strike a deal on the issue. These existing proposals thus kept on coming at the discussion table without any meaningful progress. However, the Iranian authorities welcomed the July 2011 Russian proposal. The proposal offered a systematic structure of a step by step approach and reciprocal steps from the other side which would subsequently lead to suspension of all 20% uranium enrichment activities from Iranian side, closure of Fordow nuclear facility and transfer of 20% enriched uranium to a third country, besides extending cooperation to IAEA (International Atomic Energy Agency) under the NPT and additional protocol. Since 2002, the Iranian nuclear program has remained in the attention. Although, after breaking out the controversy, especially with the revelations by the NCRI about some of the secret Iranian nuclear installations, Iran did try to do damage control by signing the additional protocol and allowing IAEA (International Atomic Energy Agency) the access to these sites, situation however changed with the election of hardliner President Ahmedinejad in 2005. (Stevens, 2014)

During his term of Presidency, Ahmedinejad not only refused to ratify the additional protocol but also stirred some further controversies by giving provocative statements about Israel, which were strongly criticized, by the Western world. Most states, including that of Israel, presumed that if Iran is on the road to acquire the nuclear weapons, which they could then use to wipe Israel of the world's map. However, this assumption was based on incorrect information and deliberate misinterpretation of President Ahmedinejad's speech by the western media. The controversy however, did evoke a strong response from the western world that resulted in diplomatic condemnation and imposition of UN sanctions. These sanctions were in addition to already imposed sanctions by the US government in 1987 by Regan administration and in 1995 by the President Bill Clinton's government. The US government added further Iranian companies and businesses to the existing list of sanctions that had adverse effects on the Iranian economy. (Rosenberg & Fox, 2013) Despite that, Iran had always maintained that these sanctions neither would hurt Iran nor would compel it to change its course on the nuclear issue; the reality appears to be somewhat different. Not only these sanctions seriously affected the Iranian economy, it also brought flexibility on the Iranian stance over its nuclear issue, especially after the change of the hard line government since 2005, (Bahgat, 2006) which finally resulted in the successful signing of the interim nuclear agreement between the P 5+1 and Iran.

According to some sources, these sanctions not only increased drastically the cost of living in Iran, thus adversely affecting the Iranian middle class, but according to official estimates, the inflation has gone up to 40% since the imposition of sanctions after 2005. Therefore, these sanctions did affect the Iranian decision making process and the hard line stance on its nuclear issue. (Pietrobon, 2013)

Impact of Israel on US-Iran Nuclear Deal

The Israeli Prime Minister Netanyahu has been among key international opponent against nuclear deal with Iran. Israel at any cost will oppose letting the nuclear deal or the nuclear capable Iran materialized. To seek international support to his explicit stance to denounce Iran's nuclear programme a severe threat to the international security. However, on the issues of nuclear deal with Iran, Israel encounters a diplomatic dilemma and having no influence to refrain the P5+1 for seeking a political resolution of the Iranian nuclear issue. Certainly, the Israel have been reluctant to embrace the nuclear deal negotiation between Iran and the P5+1 however, the US consent to set aside Iran's retention of a lingering nuclear capacity, Israel attempted every option to disrupt the process of prospective success of the deal. (Hicks & Dalton, 2017). The Israeli Prime Minister termed the announcement of JCPOA on 14 July, 2015 as a historic mistake that would only add to the sufferings and the instability of the global peace and security. Furthermore, he asserted to use all means to dissuade possibility of Iran's nuclear capability since, Israel was not bound by the deal and or the JCPOA. (Maloney, 2016).

The struggle to seek international political support for Israel against the nuclear deal with Iran is proclaimed on the grounds that it gradually has generated a sense of insecurity in minds of Israeli people that are surrounded by hostile nations. In response, Israel is only left with the option to aggressively take measures against Iran to become either a nuclear capable state or a beneficiary of the international nuclear deal. Israel pretends to be less willing with the issue of taking risks on regional security matters and potential concern pertains to Palestine, Syria and Lebanon alike. However, the use of force is not a suitable choice since it is not even in favor of Israel due to the reason fact that cost of retaliation could prove higher than the expectation. (Entessar & Afrasiabi, 2015). The only obtainable choice left for Israel is to use its political influence to diplomatically isolate Iran in the international arena and obstruct the possible success of the P5+1 nuclear deal with Iran. The political choice enables Israel to impact over the success of the nuclear deal by putting Iran in a state of isolation and political frustration but however, such a case would further keep Iran attempting to challenge the Western interest its region. Any further political isolation of Iran may become less practical due to the fact that Iran has previously been sustaining the burdens of economic sanctions and political isolation. (Rajiv, 2016)

Power Dynamics in the Region

The international advantage and the status of the nuclear capable powers greatly appeal the requiring and acquiring the nuclear technology. The nuclear weapons considered a major source of international prestige and the means of political influence and therefore, the non-nuclear weapon states have been in constant curiosity of getting the nuclear technology through their clandestine programs. The pressure by the international community particularly after the IAEA (International Atomic Energy Agency) reports released in November 2011 severely alleged Iran for its continuation of the clandestine nuclear program. Moreover, IAEA (International Atomic Energy Agency) complained about Iran's uncooperative attitude toward inspection. The non-cooperative attitude gives an impression of Iran's unwillingness for stopping its nuclear technology activities ("Iran deal in doubt?" 2015)

The inspection team reported that Iran is not fulfilling its responsibilities as a signatory of additional protocol of NPT. Iran maintained an ambiguous stance regarding its nuclear programme. The report hints towards the wrong intention Iran has, which means that Iran is making or intends to make the nuclear weapons in future. The reports of inspection proved the claims of the USA and Israel right that Iran is on the way towards like nuclear weapons. As a result of these reports the USA and UNO imposed intense sanctions on Iran, which were very productive in shaping Iranians behavior towards its nuclear programme. The effect of the sanctions on the behavior of Iranian people could be trace to the results in the election of 2013, whereas people elected moderates and progressive minded leadership, who were expected to shows flexibility on the nuclear issue. That flexible and soft stance of new Iranian leader ultimately led to a successful deal between Iran and world community. (Burr & Byrne, n.d)

The prolong controversy over Iran's nuclear program and the conflicts in the region previously put Iran in a highly delicate situation where at one side it faced severe international economic sanctions, threats of invasion and at the other hand a regional pressure by its rivals in the neighborhood. The traditional alliance between the US and the Arab countries of the region and the recent nuclear deal with Iran depicts the prospective symbolism that is going to take place amidst the regional power shift. Though not progressing towards the acquisition of the nuclear weapons however, the economic power though oil and natural gas resources are going to become the source of place for Iran to hold the dominant and to some extent a hegemonic position in the regional context.

The idea of development of relationship and eventually an alliance in future between Iran and the United States could boost up the transitional process of power shift in the region. Iran in that case will have a leading role and support the US in getting upper hand over the issues and interests that were uncontrollable before. For instance, the Iranian side will keenly tackle the security issues in Afghanistan and the rise of extremist Sunni group like

ISIS. Moreover, the Iran-US nexus could hamper new avenues and opportunities for the Central Asian Republics.

The close proximity of the Iranian geographic location and the trade and resource potential support the Western objectives of pulling back the Central Asian states out of the Russian influence. Besides the regional alliance such as the Shanghai Cooperation Organization (SCO) and the Commonwealth of Independent States (CIS), the Russian Federation has been enjoyed an edge than any other state in the region. The traditional sphere of Russian influence in the Central Asia and Eurasia could be receding with an exceptionally vibrant foreign policy and the economic potential of Iran. However, the conventional support for each other's stance between the Iran and Russia could not prevent a regional competition focusing on deliberate attainment of vital national interests entirely change the political, economic and the security narrative about Iran's role and influence in the regional affairs. (Bardes, Shelley, & Schmidt, 2014) The Arab world looking towards the US for their security needs creates a split between both sides particularly due to the opportunities that come underway for Iran after the prospectively successful nuclear deal. The revenues earned by Iran through exports of its rich oil and natural gas resources, the strategic tools of Iran such as Hezbollah and other militant groups become more powerful than ever before. The historical rivalry and the ideological confrontation between the Sunni Arab and the Shiite Iran is another reason that pushes the two sides for further propagation and the hegemony in the surroundings. The two sides have been immensely contributing their financial support for their respective pro-ideology groups that auxiliary execute and shore up respective schools of thought. (Jackson, 2009)

Iran is one of the chief supporter for different proxies in the region to maintain its political influence and presence in form of non state actor. This role of Iran is prominent and evident in the following proxies:-

i. Iran is the only supporter of Bashar ul Assad in the region and contributing blood and money continuously to the Syrian civil war and rebel groups

ii. Iran threatening the Israel's security through its support for Hezbollah militants.

iii. Iran is providing financial and material support to the Houthi rebels of Saudi Arabian backed government of Yemen. Iran is also allegedly involved in providing CDCM launches.

The recent restlessness in many countries like Syria, Yemen, Iraq, Bahrain, Tunisia and even Pakistan is the compact reason of conflicts, confrontation and the civil wars that eventually and abruptly become a rationale for conflagration for the social structure of these countries. The Arab-Iran confrontation with the tools of pondering huge amounts of money merely for the dominance of their respective ideology that in turn contemplation would provide these countries an edge for predominantly holding an upper hand over the national and foreign policy making process of aforementioned countries. In some situations, the case remained totally vice-versa since the traditional rivalry between the Sunni and Shiite groups though prevail in the Middle East and the Levant region but the exceptional uncertainty for the regimes of failing states came through the rise of Sunni militias against their regimes. Many other groups regardless of their ideological differences also joined hands with the rebel groups of against the rulers. For instance, the removal of President Hussn-e-Mobarak's regime in Egypt was a result of collective protest and violent rebel of Sunni and Shiite masses of Egypt. ("Gulf Politics and Economics in a Changing World", 2014) The transitional phase as a consequence of the prospective success also enables Iran to portray designs of regional salience further becoming obvious since its exceptional geostrategic location that Iran enjoys. The current geostrategic location enables Iran to be a significant player in the regional affairs. All of this makes Iran a role model for many states who has rapidly progressed despite facing immense challenges. Iran is holding the Strait of Hormuz in Persian Gulf which is one of the key positions in term of international trade and supply of oil. Iran considers itself the custodian of Shiite ideology and revolutions. Iran supports, sometime diplomatically and sometimes militarily, different Shiite groups in many important countries in the region. The countries with Iranian supported groups include Iraq, Pakistan, Bahrain, Lebanon, and Yemen.

Previously, the nuclear option was main objective for the Iranian side to increase the opportunities of its success for the policy attainment has ultimately shifted to the increasingly dominate the regional affairs through economic tools and the power. The nuclear deal between the US and Iran do not promise a firm occasion of total lift of sanctions nevertheless, a marginal draw down in the sanctions obviously may become an opportunity to gradually increase its involvement and the role in the international political and economic discourse. ("International politics of the Persian Gulf", 2012)

The conservative perspective is emphasizing over skepticism of the gradually increasing role of Iran in the regional and international issues but the moderate outlays about the augmented influence of Iran portray novel opportunities underway. The sanction lift is perceived as a major breakthrough is removing the obstacles amidst the way of Iran to holdup economic and political supremacy viz a viz to its rival Gulf countries ("U.S.-Iran nuclear deal could shift regional power," 2016)

4 IRAN NUCLEAR DEAL AND POWER DYNAMICS FOR IRAN AND SAUDI ARABIA

The proxy forces usually never bear a label of any particularly country but are essentially considered as strategic assets and can be employed when ever and where in case of rise of any conflict like situation in the region. However, apart from the stopping the acquisition of nuclear technology, the conditional nuclear deal also limits Iran's role and policies in supporting its traditional allies in Syria, Iraq, Bahrain, Yemen and Lebanon. The political pressure can cast drastic influence over Iran, as a consequence of ignorance would once again threaten Iran's progression and the goals national buildup and the growing participation and the role in the international affairs. Similarly, during the initial stage of the nuclear deal with Iran, the United States also came under severe criticism by its traditional allies that enthusiastically enquired the implication that encouraged the Obama administration to jot down this deal with Iran and bypass all the concerns and prevailing regional security and political dynamics. The closest ally of the United States, Israel repeatedly tried with stern efforts to hamper the possibility of the nuclear deal with Iran. The Israeli Prime Minister Benjamin Netanyahu termed the nuclear deal with

Iran as one of the most drastic and dangerous mistakes of the history that the civilized world has never witnessed before. The Saudi Arabia also slammed the US-Iran nuclear deal on the grounds that it would be nothing more than pushing the already suffering Middle Eastern region towards further chaos and conflicts merely creating wreaks for the havoc. (Samore & Allison, n.d.) All the power competitor of the region namely Iran, Israel, and Saudi Arabia has respective aspirations to influence and dominate the region through their military and economic power. This has resulted in an ongoing competition and power struggle within the region that is affecting the regional security matrix. Although Arab states have shown concerns about Israel's nuclear weapons, which all know virtually exists, however; the uneven relations of Arab countries with Iran also favor Israel's position in the regional milieu. The hostile relations between Arab states and Iran are benefiting the Israel to enhance its role in the region. Israel is the only country in the region which can change is the equation of balance of power in the region.

Balance of Power Before Nuclear Deal

The rivalry between Saudi Arabia and Iran is not only geopolitical in nature but it has other dimensions as well. There are many historical, sectarian and economic dimensions of rivalry, which could fuel any conflicts between the two states. The rivalry between Iran and Saudi Arabia is rooted in their bitter history and sectarian division which further evolved into geopolitical competition in the Middle Eastern region. The rivalry raises several concerns which are diplomatic, economic, political, security etc.

The role of Saudi Arabia increased with the propagation of Wahabism school of thought and the exporting of the ideology to the Arab and some Asian countries. The Royal regime of Saudi Arabia declared themselves the custodian of the holy sites in the country and consequently the leaders of the Muslim world. There are several recent events and accidents related to the Middle East that brought some radical changes in the power dynamics of the region, in the aftermath of 9/11 terror attacks in the US, US-Iraq war 2003, Arab uprising and the US-Iran nuclear deal. The US attack on Iraq in 2003 and the resulting removal of Saddam Hussain from the political scene of Middle East changed the whole security arrangements of the region because he was a balancing force against Iran in the region. (Ballengée, 2015) The Arab uprisings destabilized the region including Syria and Egypt and strengthen the non-state actors and proxies, mostly supported and sponsored by both Saudi Arab and Iran. It also showed to the Arab regimes, including Saudi Arab, that their kingdoms are not infallible. All these developments played very important role in reducing the role of Saudi Arabia and strengthening the role of Iran in the region.

The successful inking of the US-Iran nuclear deal in July, 2015 opened a new era of diplomatic and international relations for Iran with the international community especially the USA and Western countries. Saudi Arabia views the rapprochement of the international community with Iran as a threat to their interests in the region which increases the hostilities in the region between Iran and Saudi Arabia. The main concern of Saudi Arabia is the support of Iran for proxies in the region, which is undermining its own influence in the region. It was Saudi Arabian concern about growing influence and support of Iran for Yemen's rebels which lead to military intervention by Royal family. Iran and Saudi Arabia are confronting each other through different means and proxies in different parts of the region, for example Syria, Yemen, Bahrain, and Iraq to enhance their influence. The Iranian support for proxies through military hardware is more strong and effective as compared to Saudi Arabian support for proxies through money and western military hardware which comes with several strings attached. (Hurd, 2015). The US-Iran nuclear deal can exceptionally impact on the dynamic regional balance of power in the favor of Iran after its successful implementation. Saudi Arabia has clearly expressed its concerns regarding the US-Iran nuclear deal and can increase its support of other proxies in the region against Iranian influence which can consequently further destabilize the already fragile Middle Eastern region. These developments in the region are leading to further intensify the already very active foreign policy of both states against each other.

Geopolitical Impact of the US-Iran Nuclear Deal

The geopolitical landscape of the Middle East and the Gulf region is underway of a major geopolitical shift in the coming future. In the pre US-Iran nuclear deal scenario, the most of the time assumption about the Iran was usually a state despite geographically present in the region is eventually out of all the economic and political affairs of the region. The Arab countries and the United States throughout the course of isolated Iran scenario managed and enjoyed greater influence over the Middle Eastern affairs. The alliance between the Arab world and the United States historically demonstrates a mix of trust, mistrust, ambiguity, and uncertainty. Ironically, the interdependence of the both side on each other eventually creates necessary circumstances to carry out their relationship by either way. The Arab world mainly looks towards the United States for the sake of their security reasons. This exceptionally enables the US to hold a position at its best. Moreover, the deployment of the US troops and holding air bases in most of the Arab countries create a sense of sanctuary and a security shelter by the regimes of Arab states. Likewise, the Arab world is a huge market of the US military equipment with ever-growing demands of the latest weaponry, warships and jet fighters. (Einhorn, n.d.)

US-IRAN NUCLEAR DEAL: POWER DYNAMICS FOR IRAN AND SAUDI ARABIA

The Arab world is particularly skeptical about the future of the regional geopolitical shift that apparently favors the Iranian side more than the Sunni Arab states. The reaction to the nuclear deal from and within the Arab world is more political in its nature. The recent shock of the Arab spring and the prevailing conflicts in the region cause a severe degree of unease to the regimes of Gulf countries. Since the inception of the US-Iran nuclear deal, the Obama administration has been assuring its traditional allies that the nuclear deal by no means would change the geopolitical impact of the region. Moreover, the members of the Gulf Cooperation Council (GCC) i.e. UAE, Saudi Arabia, Kuwait, Qatar, Oman and Bahrain by no means offset and equal to the influence of Iran in the region. The soft corner of Iran for Hezbollah, Hamas, Kurdish Peshmerga forces and many other militant groups is a reason of resentment for the Turkey and Iraq besides the vulnerable posture of the Arab countries. The situation in the post-Saddam Hussein Iraq is more inclined towards and greatly favors Iran in the regional security architecture. Furthermore, the Egypt has been considered an iron grip and one of the militarily powerful states of the Arab world and has remained a potentially traditional rival of the Iran. However, the domestic chaotic situation along with political de-stability and the economic crises are the some of the potential reasons that never allow the Egypt to create a conventional counterweight and sustain an established leading position of against Iran in the regional context. (Mousavian, 2014) The geopolitical situation in the post Iran-US nuclear deal scenario has shown an abrupt aggressive response from the Arab world. The less acceptable approach is an outcome of the Iran has alleged involvement in the regional security issues more specifically, the Arab countries have been alleged Iran in its clandestine role of sponsoring the uprisings against their regimes.

The prevailing delicate situation of the Arab regimes makes them further vulnerable and hard to face any further chaos. The current scenario of political dissection within the Gulf Cooperation Council will further favor Iran due to the external security dependence of the Gulf countries. The nuclear deal would bring an end to the political isolation of Iran rather it will further increase its role in the regional and international political and security affairs that would of course significantly gradient and eventually shift the regional balance of power towards the Iranian side. The eager pursuance of the political objectives by the Saudi Arabia may drastically help in overcoming the existing delicate situation and help in balancing the power equilibrium against Iran. However, the lack of trust regarding the US policies during the Syria crisis is the main factor further adding to the concerns of the Arab countries. The prevailing sentiment of the Arab countries similarly depicts the views of reaction by the West merely for the attainment of their own policy agendas. (Herzog, n.d.) The other view about the geopolitical shift amidst a successful Iran-US nuclear deal would prove otherwise contradictory to the Saudi Arabia's exaggerated fears the possible outcome would be more optimistic having high ratio of opportunities for the whole region. Iran portrays and demonstrates the increased options of cooperation between the Gulf Countries rather than hegemonic designs favoring any particular side. Apart from the question of Arab-Iran tension, there are other regional competitors like Turkey that may not feel easy with the Iran's rise. The role of Iran in the Syria crisis and Iraq also demonstrates uneven relationship in the near future between Iran and Turkey. The Saudi-Turkey nexus in the regional security milieu also seems an effort to counter the growing influence of Iran.

The Iranian regime is also extremely sensitive towards the Palestinian issue, probably of its ideological rivalry with the state of Israel since the Islamic

Revolution of 1979. Iran, prior to the revolution enjoyed extremely friendly and cordial relations with the state of Israel, however, the equation completely changed just after Ayatollah Khomeini seized the power. The current Iranian government has openly and categorically termed the Israeli government as illegitimate and unacceptable thus adopting an extremely hostile attitude towards the state of Israel. The Iran-Israel relations usually contradictory while seeming through the ideological lens but Iran's relations with other states like those that India are generally base upon the notion of pragmatism and merely focusing on the attainment of hardcore national interests. (Erhieyovwe, & Onokero, 2013)

The recently concluded interim deal between the P–5+1 and Iran are also attributed towards the Iranian pragmatic approach in which the US also showed flexibility despite serious reservations from Israel. Consequently, some scholars think that the change of face in Tehran after the elections of 2013 has dramatically changed the regional scenario and has thus brought some hope for the future stability and peace in the region. Similarly, the antagonist speculates at first proclaim Iranian nuclear deal would prove counterproductive in view that it would enable Iran to buy time to consolidate over its nascent nuclear expertise. Besides igniting sectarian tensions as majority of the Sunni states in the region might not accept the reality of a nuclear armed Iran and consequently start nuclear programs of their own, thus leading to regional nuclear proliferation. (Flanagan & Wall, n.d.) The Gulf Cooperation Council (GCC) holds serious concerns about Iranian nuclear program and intentions. Although, they are not in good terms with Israel and the nuclear programme of Israel is not acceptable to the Arab states but the threat of Iran nuclear programme is also diverting the attention of Arab states from Israel to Iran. There is a clear sectarian divide between Iran and Arab states along with bitter historical events.

Sunny Arab states consider the sectarian and historical divide with Iran more significant and threatening than Israel. The nuclear-armed Israel is not considered a big threat to the Arab world and therefore acceptable. On the other hand, the Arab states believe that a nuclear armed Iran will significantly change the political and security arrangements of the Middle Eastern region. However, these states are also struck with the dilemma, as on one side these states want Iran to be stopped from acquiring a capability, which it could use to develop the nuclear weapons. Even if entails a military strike, but they also know that if such a strike ever takes place either by the US or Israel, it would push the region towards more violence and instability.

Their situation can be equated with a scenario of being trapped between the devil and the deep sea. The GCC and the western states share the concern that nuclear capability would give Iran a leverage to dictate its terms in the region which could further incite the sectarian rivalries and would cause problems for the Sunni monarchies which happens to be the main exporters of the oil to the Europeans and the US (Blockmans, Ehteshami, & Bahgat, n.d.)

Acquiring of the nuclear weapon by one state could stimulate other nations for acquiring nuclear technology for themselves. This will ultimately led to a nuclear arms race in the region. In case of Iran gaining the nuclear weapons, the militant groups in the region would be dictated by Iran without considering major consequences from other regional states. This whole situation will strengthen especially those groups which are engaged in gorilla fight in Lebanon against somewhat periodic Israeli invasions. In such a situation not only the role of regional countries but the western powers would also be very limited in the regional politics. In past, the Arab states were less aggressive towards Iran and disapprove any military solution of the matter. (Mason, 2016)

US-IRAN NUCLEAR DEAL: POWER DYNAMICS FOR IRAN AND SAUDI ARABIA

The US quest to isolate Iran through diplomatic and economic means have not proved entirely successful as Iran has effectively used its oil as a weapon to dodge these sanctions by offering Asian economic giants cheap oil than the international markets. Iran has relied on economic diplomacy to improve its relations with the regional states, a trend which has changed amid the transforming the regional landscape after the revolutions in some of the Arab states which were coined as Arab Spring. (Parisi & Esfandiary, n.d.)

Whereas, the Saudis fear that any change in the government of Bahrain could drastically reduce the Saudi influence in the country, which could thus affect the Saudi stature in the region at the cost of rising Iranian influence. Some diverse views also proclaim about the Saudi Arabia's longing for a serious option by the US to overcome the threat at any cost but it will drastically increase the support of Islamic countries in favor of the Iran. To resolve the issue of Iran nuclear programme, it is believed that the military strike would not be as much helpful. The US and its allies are equally concerned with the aftermath of any military strike against Iran as it could further worsen the situation. This will enable Iran to gather more sympathies of Muslim masses around the world. (Blockmans, Ehteshami, & Bahgat, n.d.)

The conclusion of recent deal between P 5+1 and Iran came as a surprise to Saudi Arabia who has discontentedly reacted over this deal. Although the subsequent reaction of the GCC states was optimistic and welcoming on the deal, but the frustration over leaving the issue open ended is obvious. This attitude of the GCC states, especially the Saudis, is indicative of the fact that Saudis want a permanent and solid solution of Iran's nuclear program.

The Transitional phase and the possibility of Prospective Success

The impulsive of nominal functionality of the outstanding symbol of Arabs power, the Arab League is practicability remained of a very less role. Once, the Arab world experienced craves of concord and power while Arab League flourished towards its zenith. The eventual outcome of Arab League's failure also resulted in the countenance of many failed states with mostly coming under direct dominance of the Sunni extremist groups.

The Syrian crises have also so far proved to become a ground that brought both Russia and Iran on the same page for their perspectives on the regional security and fight against the radical groups such as Islamic State of Iraq and Syria (ISIS). The rise of extremist groups like ISIS has been collectively perceived a major threat as a whole to the international community. Notably, all the states coping with the rise of extremist groups and the ISIS have their respective interests and agendas in doing so. For instance, the interests of Turkey vary than the interest of Iraq or Syria. Apart from the ongoing difference in the context of strategic interest there are manifold chances that the anti-ISIS forces including Iran, Turkey, Iraq, Hezbollah and the Kurdish Peshmerga may form an alliance to counter the rise and threat of the militant group. ("Iran-Turkey nuclear deal looks uncertain" 2013) Although their rampant ideological difference however, as a collective interest all the stakeholders and the Arab countries like Egypt, Yemen, Saudi Arabia and the UAE may also form a collective response and join the communal response in the near future. The regional rapprochement may become auxiliary benign for all these states to handle the regional issues at their behest rather than involving and looking for the support of extra-regional forces. (Mousavian, 2014)

In the aftermath of Iran nuclear deal, Russia shortly made a scaffold weapons deal with Iran. The supply of the S-300 air-defence missile system from Russia side was a proclamation of the in accordance with the United Nations Security Council's resolution 1929 that only restricts the sale of offensive military equipment to the sanctioned countries. Furthermore, the prospects of Russia-Iran military cooperation is prospectively becoming manifold since the current tension between Russia and Turkey over shot - down of Russian jet in March 2016 allegedly violating the Turkish territorial sovereignty is another political opportunity Iran would definitely cash in its favor for creating a regional nexus against the traditional competitors. In January 2016, the visit of Russian defence Minister Sergei Shoigu and the Russian call for lifting the sanctions on arms embargo and thereof the estimated sale of Russian military equipment to Iran shortly reached $13 billion. (Burr & Byrne, n.d.) Interestingly, in the short course of time, the smooth foreign policy and the diplomatic culmination of Iran have additionally resulted in the accomplishments beyond the region. The foreign policies of Israeli Prime Minister Benjamin Netanyahu, for instance have created a trudge in the antagonism against his country. This for case in point has turned in favor of Iran and a drastic shift in Israeli propaganda has eventually resulted in the shape of a soft image about Iran has been emerging amongst the international community of nations. (Mousavian, 2014)

The economic and trade potential of Iran is further twisted out of the lifting of sanctions and the European nations eagerly look for the bilateral deals with Iran. In addition, a mix of feelings pushes the Western nations to explore an alternative source of oil and natural gas they depend upon Russia. Besides Western antagonism, the Russian Federation recently signed a bilateral agreement with the Islamic Republic for the initial supply of half a million barrels of crude oil that would be refined and sold by Russia in the international market. In turn, the Russian accord with Iran for construction of two nuclear power reactors depicts a regional effort for undermining and preventing the possible external involvement in the spheres of predominant powers' influence. (Mousavian, 2014)

Unlike the political backdrop of many regimes in the Gulf and the Middle Eastern countries, the rise of Iran as a region's unwavering power is likely to be acceptable to most of the countries in the region. The leading role could be an unforeseen opportunity for the Iranian side since the successful transitional process from a sanctioned conservative and so-called rogue nation of the world is going to become exceptionally vibrant and gaining a key place in the community of the civilized nations of the world. The successful deal between Iran and the P5+1 could bring an end to the 35 year long standoff that in turn gave nothing to Iran but only sufferings to its people and an isolated place in the international affairs. The prospective position of Iran in the near future also unfolds tremendous opportunities for its traditional allies, partners and the states in the region. The sort of opportunity may vary in its nature. Some of the states in the region may benefit from the trade transaction coming into their way through Iran and the Western exports. Whereas, the traditional partners and allies of Iran may get immense in terms of diverse option encompassing the areas from military, economic and the political advantages.

The usual argument about Iran's nuclear program is an intentional move to stop its nuclear programme. According to the views maintained by the Iranian political leadership and religious clergy that maintaining ambiguous stance about nuclear programme can produce more political and economic advantages for Iran rather than a clear and vivid stance on the issue. They also give as a reference the success of ambiguous stand of Israel on its own nuclear program. They believe that they can advance their interests in the international community while having nuclear programme as a bargaining tool. The Iranian quest for the nuclear weapon is not only for the purpose of its defense but also for imposing aggressive foreign policy in the region to increase its influence and at the end establish its hegemony. (Miller, 2008)

The concerns of Israel also may be justified on the grounds that the nuclear deal with Iran would cause a tremendous imbalance of regional power equilibrium and the status-quo change abruptly. However, the unfavorable circumstances do not trail Israeli wishes of rolling back of an international nuclear deal with Iran is a bitter reality. For Israel, the ray of hope may become close cooperation with the Arab countries since both share common agenda and a common threat from Iran rise and power. The Previous Iranian threats to the Jewish state for eliminating it from the world map though may not have changed nevertheless; the international political pressure and the recent role of Iran in the global political milieu would of course restrain it from showing apparently hostile attitude towards not only Israel but also any regional or extra-regional state in the world. The tag of a responsible state over Iran also demand many other compromises on its support to the proxy militias, financing likeminded ideological groups in various countries and sponsoring any uprising in the Arab world. (Parisi & Esfandiary, n.d.)

The European nations are also particularly concerned about the nuclear proliferation issue in the Middle East. Being in close proximity, they realize that in case of an Iranian nuclear weapon, the tensions in Middle East would rise which is already passing through a delicate stage and thus would affect the regional stability which could have drastic implications for the already ailing economy. More so the Europeans states claim that their concerns with regards to Iran are not just country specific but rather are aimed at efforts in preventing a general proliferation within and outside the region. The P5+1 states are also inclined towards finding a peaceful solution to the Iranian nuclear issue whereas the Israelis have always been trying to persuade the US for taking a military action against Iran. These states are concerned that a nuclear armed Iran could change the regional balance and thus could harm their interests in the region. Israel already has the nuclear weapons, therefore in their opinion, a nuclear armed Iran could increase the risk of a nuclear exchange because the militant groups like Hezbollah, Hamas and Islamic Jihad etc. could feel emboldened to launch more active operations against Israel who could react with brute force resulting in hundreds of civilian casualties and could provoke Iran to use the nuclear weapons as a justifiable mean to punish Israel. It was primarily the efforts of the European states and the flexibility shown by the Ruhani regime which resulted into finalization of the interim nuclear deal with Iran. (Porter, n.d.) This nuclear deal has significantly reduced the dangers of a military strike on Iranian nuclear installations and is likely to built trust between the opposing parties which could prove to be helpful for further negotiations and finding a permanent solution to the burning issue.

Iran's Economic Rebound

In case the interim nuclear deals fail to achieve the desired objectives and the peaceful solution towards Iranian nuclear crisis becomes would of course drag Iran into further economic chaos. Since the oil and natural resources of Iran besides huge trade potential, it would hardly find any customer state to be ready to buy despite international economic sanction. Moreover, the failure of the deal would also invite improbable the military strikes would naturally be sought by Israel either with or even without the US support. (Ellner, 2013) Failure of deal would create a deep crisis for the whole world as the oil prices could climb massively and the oil supplies could be disrupted thus shaking the already fragile global economy to its foundations. States feeling unease from thought of a nuclear-armed Iran could heavily invest in the arms deals that could result in cutting expenditures in other important sectors like health, education, power generation etc, thus affecting the overall economic growth.

The world is still facing the adverse economic effects of the war in Iraq, the Libyan conflict and the civil war in Syria. These wars have created a deeply disturbing humanitarian crisis in shape of refugees and food shortages. People in these affected areas are trying to settle in other peaceful regions thus creating flux of asylum seekers and illegal immigrants trying to reach Europe, Australia and even America. This situation is thus forcing these western states in different continents to spend more on their internal surveillance and border security measures that have a continuous recurring cost for the economy. Thus another conflict or the nuclear weapon capability in the hands of Iran could just create the right conditions which could have devastating implications for the regional and global economy.

Defensive realist posits the most intuitive reason for pursuing nuclear arms; a state believes its security is threatened and seeks to reduce the threat through acquisition of a nuclear deterrent. This can involve allying with a nuclear capable state or self-sufficiency in terms of nuclear capability. Although, there is no dearth of scholars who believe that Iranian nuclear ambitions in the region are not defensive but offensive. The Iranians primarily wants to establish their regional hegemony in the region through which not only Iran wants a greater regional role but also a decisive say in the regional politics. They cite the Iranian support to Hezbollah, Iranian involvement with Syria and its increasing role in the Iraqi domestic politics, as evidence of Iranian regional reach and ambitions. The economic rebound of Iran may also trigger a regional arms race in terms the proxy militant groups cause trouble in many states and instigate the chaos against the ruling monarch of many Arab states in the region. However, the economic prosperity most prospectively may also benefit all the states in the region. The manifold trade and economic opportunities for the states in the region can circulate the immense finances for all regardless of any alliance or enmity. (Dupont, 2013)

The current controversy over the Iranian nuclear program became divisive after the exposing the underground sites of Arak and Natanz in 2002 by National Council of Resistance of Iran. This disclosure raised many questions about the nature and aspects of Iran nuclear programme especially the existence of possible aspect of making nuclear bomb.

Iran is gradually mastering the nuclear fuel cycle technology and increasing its expertise in nuclear technology especially in enriching the uranium. Iranian claim that its advancement in the nuclear technology aimed at impressing the world about its national capabilities, technological advancement appears dubious, and controversial, as western states have accused that Iran has intentions to develop the nuclear weapons and thus has kept its some of the sites hidden from the world community. (G, 2012)

Improvement in the US-Iran Relations

The issue of Iran's nuclear program and capability has involved the regional countries and Western powers in a controversy. The issue focuses on Iran's nuclear ambitions and potential capability. Iran argues that using nuclear technology for the peaceful purpose its right, which cannot be denied. They claim that its nuclear programme is for purpose of its future need of energy due to the depleted sources of its energy, however, International Atomic Energy Agency IAEA shows its concerns regarding dubious and suspicious nuclear activities. Tehran is the member of NPT, the United States intelligence reports also claimed that its programme is suspicious. United States, Israel and EU are also of the opinion that Tehran is moving towards the nuclear weapon but on the other hand the Tehran's officials are denying it and claiming that its nuclear programme is for peaceful purpose, which will meet its future demand for energy (Forouzanfar, Goghary, & Daryabaygi, 2014)

For some obvious reasons, the US response had been to check Iran's regional ambitions. In the US position, if Iran pursues the nuclear weapons program, it will not advance Iran's security, spark an arms race in the region causing instability. Iranian nuclear weapon possession will not be acceptable to the US. In addition, the US has the option to deploy weapons to its established strategy of extended deterrence. With this strategy, the US can limit the influence of Iran in the region. On the other hand, Russia and China can be important to help fight the proliferation of the nuclear weapons. However, the US collaboration with these states can increase pressure on Iran. Russia and China can play a role to prevent Iran from the nuclear weapons quest. However, Russia and China seem to have different perceptions of Iran's nuclear threat. (Arnold, 2014)

The Gulf countries have potential to have their own nuclear weapon capability to balance the effect of a nuclear-Iran. This will start a nuclear arms race in the region that increases the chances of nuclear war. Similarly, Iranian alleged support for non-state actors for implementation of its objectives in the region can lead to a dangerous situation leading to crisis with a nuclear dimension. Iran is continuously working on improving its military strength based on a nuclear capability. The regional politics is also important in this regard, as there are several atomic powers like Pakistan, India, China, Russia and Israel. Iran has strong feelings that only the nuclear weapons can secure its national integrity in the future. Presence of the US and NATO troops in Afghanistan and the US' military bases in the Gulf and Central Asia are posing a security challenge for Iran. The US is keen to implement its containment strategy to halt Iran's nuclear quest. Other major powers are also trying to reach an understanding with Iran over the nuclear issue. The US and its allies are perceiving threats from terrorist groups in Iraq and Afghanistan. Of course, Iranian support is not clear but the US intelligence agencies are accusing Iran for its military support to non-state actors. If Iran becomes a nuclear-armed state the threat of nuclear terrorism can affect the US objectives in the region. Thus, the United States strategy of Iranian isolation from the international community and stopping its nuclear program seems rational. ("Unthinkable: Iran, the bomb, and American strategy," 2014)

In response to Iranian nuclear issue, the United States has embarked on a series of economic and diplomatic sanctions. Moreover, the EU and UNSC also supported the strategy of isolation and sanctioning Iran. However, there is need to do more as sanctions regime is not adequate to limit Iranian nuclear activities. The United Nations and Europeans are banning Iranian exports of oil and gas to strengthen the sanctions regime. This led to further standoff between Iran and the west especially the USA. However, China, Russia and even Europe are showing reluctance over strict punitive economic sanctions. Pakistan, although supported international sanctions regime, has shown concern over ban on Iranian oil and gas exports due to country's energy requirements. Iranian nuclear weapon would provide Iran credible nuclear deterrence. However, the west questions the rationality of Iranian leadership. At times, Iranian behavior is aggressive towards the west. The United States would need to extend nuclear guarantees towards its Gulf region allies to meet the Iranian threat. This would reduce the impact of the global nuclear non-proliferation regime. Still many states are pressurizing the US to take serious steps to halt Iran's nuclear activities.

In case of any military strike against Iranian nuclear sites would turn into as an emerging threat to regional security. Iran will be ready for a robust response. Therefore, the use of force considered last option for the Iranian nuclear issue. Failure of western diplomacy could eventually lead them to military option because Iran is using delay-tactics through diplomacy and time-consuming negotiations. In these circumstances, Iran's strategy to gain time is probably to push its' nuclear program. Strict measures are required from the non-proliferation regime. The NPT, Review Conferences, IAEA (International Atomic Energy Agency) inspections, implementation of UNSC Resolutions and other international actions would restrict Iran from the nuclear weapons quest. Strict actions would probably serve Iranian compliance with international obligations. To address Iranian reservations, it would probably help the international community to resolve the nuclear issue once for all. (Gyngell, 2009) Iran views its uranium enrichment facilities are part of its civilian nuclear program but the west denies Iran's claim. Although Iran's nuclear energy program is under the umbrella of Nuclear Non-Proliferation Treaty (NPT), but IAEA (International Atomic Energy Agency) has serious reservations that Iran found in non-compliance with its NPT safeguard agreements. As the situation has not improved, regional security seems under strain. A resolution can come through diplomacy that addressed the Iran's security interests as well as western concerns over Iran's nuclear quest.

There is yet no consensus that whether Iran actually wants to develop the nuclear weapons or there are other possible motives behind its calculated move to escalate the crisis. The first assumption on the Iranian rhetoric is that Iran just wants to remain at the threshold of developing the nuclear weapons while not actually crossing the redline, which would keep its stakes high within the international community and enable Iran to remain in a strong bargaining position. The other group of scholars conceives that Iran is actually worried about its security especially after having witnessed the fate of Afghanistan, Iraq and Libya, and the only possibility to avoid such a fate is to have a nuclear deterrent of its own. These scholars also see the North Korean decision of withdrawing from the NPT and testing a nuclear device in the same very context. The third group of scholars, actually very less in umber, regard Iranian nuclear program is solely meant for the power generation due to depleting oil and gas reserves in the Gulf region. Therefore, the Western fears regarding Iranian nuclear program not only lacks credibility but also blown out of proportion due to Israeli fears. Similarly, the IAEA relationship with Iran has remained very potholed. The Western influence on the agency is well known thus its attitude towards Iran and Pakistan have been different from that of Israel. Despite that there was never a conclusive evidence of Iran actively pursuing a nuclear weapons program, yet punitive sanctions were imposed on Iran over the IAEA reports, which were allegedly prepared under the US and western pressures. The IAEA also remained successful in getting the additional protocol signed from Iran which although could not be got ratified due to the unexpected change of the Iranian government in 2005. However, since the change in the US government, the current administration despite under heavy Israeli pressure has changed its policies towards Iran using a mix of sanctions and promised rewards. This US approach helped the IAEA to successfully negotiate an interim nuclear deal with Iran that is seen as a first step towards resolving the Iranian nuclear issue through peaceful means. (Jefferson, 2005). The Overall impact of the Iranian nuclear weapon on the non-proliferation could be negative. However, the fears of a nuclear domino effect look less probable. The states, which are not enjoying very cordial relations with Iran like Saudi Arabia, Qatar, and Bahrain, might rely more on the global powers like the US. The vastly discussed issue of Iran and the WMDs virtually depicts a pragmatic approach by the Iranian leadership. Nuclear program of Iran is facing a lot of challenges because Iran is located in a very less integrated and volatile part of Middle Eastern region where Israel, the strategic partner of the USA is already equipped with the nuclear weapons. The pressure of the West, especially of the US, against Iran is not only due to its nuclear activities, but also due to its the Middle East policies that stand in deep contradiction with those of the US. Factors such of the Iran's support for Hamas and Hezbollah, rejection of the existence of Israel, pressure of nuclear Israel in the Middle East with the US support. The US presence around Iran in Afghanistan, Iraq and the Gulf, are some causes of strong concern for Iran. ("Spying on the bomb: American nuclear intelligence from Nazi Germany to Iran and North Korea," 2007)

President of National Iranian American Council has an optimistic view regarding normalization of Iran relations with west after the nuclear deal, which will reduce the burden of sanctions and pressure on Iran. President NIAC said that the nuclear deal will bring positive changes in future; he proclaimed the possibilities of interaction between the USA and Iran for achieving common interest and goal.

SAJID MAHMOOD KHAN

Iran Nuclear Deal and Saudi Arabia: The Balance of Power

For most of Arab States especially Saudi Arabia, a nuclear-armed Iran is viewed as a Shiite bomb. The rulers of regional Sunni monarchies are particularly concerned since this scenario would definitely strengthen the Iranian regional stature that seeks aspirations from its old historical legacy. Such dominating nuclear power in the region could encourage Iran to export its old ambition of exporting the Shiite influence form outside its borders through proxies, an aim that set forth by the Iranian revolutionary leader Ayatollah Khomeini. Such issues could further escalate the rivalries between the Shiite and Sunni states and consequently affect the whole region and as such, this situation would incite tensions among other states especially Pakistan, Bahrain and Saudi Arabia etc.

Due to the uprising and transformation of the Middle East the Saudi Arabia is worried about its policy of maintaining the status quo at internal as well as regional level. Iran and Saudi Arabia are traditional rival and competitor in the region suspects each as a security threat. Both the countries are in constant state of threat and insecurity. The competition of both states for achieving their security is not only limited to internal arrangements as well as external steps. Therefore this security dilemma lead states to respond with strict measures. Saudi Arabian regime is concerned about the influence of Islamic revolution not only in the Middle East but also inside the Saudi Arabia. This scenario led Saudi Arabia to increase her relations with western power especially the USA to address the concerns of Saudi Arabia regarding Iran's influence. Iran is seeking the role of regional actors in attaining security and wants arrangements excluding great powers and Israel from the equation. Saudi Arabia is seeking the role of western powers including Israel to reshape the regional order and isolate Iran economically and politically. Saudi Arabia is currently worried about the growing influence of Iran in the region and shifting balance of power in the favour of Iran in the Middle East.

The growing influence of Iran is also challenging the interests of Saudi Arabia in the region and can possibly threaten its security in near future. Saudi Arabia is increasing its military strength for safeguard its interests in the region and internal stability. After successful inking of Nuclear deal between P5+1 and Iran limited the possibilities of isolating and weakening the position of Iran in the region through UN sanctions and sanctions of west.

The Arab League is much concerned about Iran's nuclear threat; Saudi Arab foreign ministry often proclaims , their nuclear programme is peaceful and is intended for energy and medical purposes. If it is true then Saudi government will not view any justification for escalation, confrontation and challenging the Iranian stand. Prince Saud Al Faisal reiterated that Iran should cooperate with Saudi Arabia to make the Persian Gulf , a nuclear free region and free of any WMD. He further said "Saudi Arabia consider Iranian nuclear programe as a threat to the stability and security of the region".

Besides the weak diplomatic relations, Saudi Arabia and Iran have a sectarian issue and therefore both states do not enjoy cordial relationship with one another. Furthermore, the assassination of Saudi ambassador Adel Al-Jubeir, in October 2011, also strained the diplomatic ties between Iran and Saudi Arabia. Other states like Iraq, Qatar, Lebanon and Yemen already facing the worsening affects of the ever-deepening sectarian rivalry would plunge into chaos. Syria, for instance already in the passing through rifts civil war which is raging between the sectarian armed groups and government forces, ruled by an Alawite off shoot of the Shiite split group.

The spillover effects of Syrian civil war are already visible in the region, whose relationship with Iran deteriorated over the latter support to Syria, Jordan, which saw some of its own massive street protests, Lebanon, where sectarian bombings are gathering pace with the passage of time. The rising sectarian violence, not only risks initiation of a regional war but would also fuel tensions within other Muslim states inside and outside the region. (Griffiths & Yadlin, 2013)

5 CONCLUSION

Findings

- The historical importance of the Middle East in the global politics is understandable due to its economic significance and energy resources. It has become a centre of conflicts, nuclear proliferation, popular upheavals and extremism. Not only the non-state actors have re-emerged from the ruins of Baghdad and Syria, the nuclear proliferation has also become a serious concern for the Western world, especially in case of Iran. The Iranian nuclear program was conceived by the Shah of Iran with apparently dubious intentions with the help of Western support. The stated purpose was to make Iran self sufficient in energy generation. However, the ambitious plan to make Iran a regional power for which nuclear weapon capability was considered as indispensable. Nevertheless, after the Islamic revolution in Iran and the Iran's war with Iraq, the Iranian nuclear program came to a standstill, as there was neither the international support nor sufficient funds to further development of nuclear power.

■ The Iran's Islamic revolution in 1979 also provoked the sectarian divisions within the Middle East thus making the whole environments extremely volatile and fragile due to Shia – Sunni divisions. These troubled and chaotic environments, coupled with the US invasion after branding Iran as a state on the axis of evil, motivated Iran to again pursue the nuclear weapon option. Not only Israel, but also the GCC states are also wary of Iranian nuclear weapon capability despite that the Iranian nuclear ambitions remains shrouded in mystery. The Israeli claims of Iran at the verge of developing the nuclear weapons have completely been proven wrong. Therefore, the US and Israeli apprehensions, that Iran could provide Hezbollah and Hamas few nuclear warheads to bomb them out, also appears to be an extremely exaggerated claim without any credible proof.

■ However, in the dominion of international politics, the prospect of Tehran's nuclear pursuit has been an important move for the regional rivalries particularly aimed at targeting the Iran. In the domain of achieving nuclear power status by Iran can bring serious changes in the Middle East and the Gulf region but will lose more with regards to vital objectives of core national interests. This change in turn would promise certain changes in the security milieu of the region where each belligerent state having its own stance on stakes. Each state besides its form of political component has respective objectives to pursue as basis of power or creating a certain level of balance of power. Iran's pursuit of nuclear technology can be conferred in the domain of having a desire to dominate the Middle Eastern region. Whereas, an Iran having successful resolution with P5+1 world powers for its nuclear issues will auxiliary change the pattern of regional politics in its favor. Moreover, the Europeans states claim that their concerns with regard to nuclear Iran are not just country specific but rather are aimed at efforts in preventing a general proliferation within and outside the region therefore, altogether put efforts in order to seek a political solution of the enduring nuclear crisis of Iran. The role of US, other nuclear power states, and the Germany have apparently drawn the sketch towards an option of peacefully overcoming the crisis.

■ The nuclear deal between Iran and P5+1 powers of the world has significantly reduced the dangers of a military escalation in the region and to some extent it can also helped in increasing the confidence amongst rival parties. The peaceful resolution of the enduring nuclear crisis of Iran could prospectively contribute to become a helpful tool for further negotiations and finding a permanent solution to the lasting regional security issues in the Middle East. The P5+1 states are also inclined towards finding a permanent and peaceful solution to the Iranian nuclear issue whereas the Israelis have always been trying to persuade the US for taking a military action against Iran. Israel and Arab states are concerned that a nuclear armed Iran could change the regional balance and thus could harm their interests in the region. The success of nuclear deal between Iran and the P5+1 states is seen as major setback for the Arab states in the region. The Arab countries and Israel having common stance against Iran. They are resolved to employ every possible option to dissuade the US administration and the global powers to refrain from the successful implementation of the nuclear deal.

■ The Iranian nuclear issue has been for the most part a highly touchy international variance since last decade. This long-drawn-out predicament has augmented apprehensions in the Middle Eastern and Gulf region, and beyond. The existence of a prolong quandary has significantly involved all the regional players including Iran in competition and race for power and hegemony in the region. The issue of nuclear deal between Iran and the

P5+1 world powers is dragged into the uncertainty since most of the Arab states are strategic partners of the US and Western powers and any deal / peaceful settlement with Iran could not appease Arab world. The suffering and chaotic Iran having less economic advantage and military means are in best interest of the Arab states. This is mainly due to the inadequate satisfaction and distrust. The nuclear deal or settlement of issues with Iran can further aggravated with the perceptions of threat emanating from the regional and international dealings on the strategic issues without taking allies in confidence. The involvement and challenging certain spheres of influence of each other by different regional actors, various events and the way they response to issues arising in their respective neighborhood has been augmenting the sentiments of Arab world about Iran. The efforts of the Arab world are aimed in directionless priorities. They are not accepting a nuclear armed Iran that could pose serious threats and undermine the core existence of the Arab states and the Israel. Secondly, Iran after having a successful nuclear deal with international powers is expand its influence by means of lifting oil trade embargo and trade relations with the other states beyond the region. In such a scenario, Iran has extra ordinary economic power and contributes to reach a prestigious position and remove its label of a rogue state.

- The lifting of economic sanction from Iran will help it in gaining significant political power and consequently more strong in terms of military strength. Despite strapping opposition through several rudiments within Iran and the US besides continuous antagonism from Israel and Saudi Arabia, the P5+1 and Iran attained an apparently enduring, wide-ranging deal acknowledged by Joint Comprehensive Plan of Action (JCPOA). This is distant from the question that promise the deal holding for its length residues uncertain, but many doubts, counting to the occurrences in the domestic politics in Iran and the US, will definitely shape its chock-full achievements.

■ It is extensively looked forward towards a tactful decree of the Iranian nuclear issue that would ultimately lead in the directions for a large-scale collaboration flanked by Iran and the Western powers. However, at hand looming fears about success of the JCPOA merely resolving the nuclear issue of Iran amidst its dealings of withdrawing the nuclear program is derivative with the question that Iran will extensive progress and contribute to the increasing tensions in near future in the region. The prevailing regional security structure takes into consideration of both options about Iran having respective status of nuclear and non-nuclear player, therefore straight away demands for essentially a sustainable pledge of the nuclear issue and enduring promise for peace in the whole region. Such an agenda is probably at stake towards the accomplishment due to recent course of events in the region particularly because of the Iranian role in the chaotic situation in the region which includes war in Syria and Yemen.

■ The world powers however, will continue pushing their respective allies towards recognizing the aspiration of long-term benefits including regional peace and exceptional opportunities of prosperity after the settlement of core issues of hostility and contention between various players of the region. In this regards, the mutually agreeable point can only be achieved through a significant role of the United Nations and facilitating all parties towards the negotiation table for successful resolution of issues through political means.

■ Throughout the course of history, Iran and the Saudi Arabia have never been easy neighbors fundamentally owing to their sectarian, political and ideological variations. The rivalry further amplified for their race of dominating the Gulf region, leading the Muslim Umma alongside their respective religious ideas and control of international energy markets. The Iranian opposition for Saudi Arabia being an ally of the extra regional powers having constant attitude of instigating the international sentiment against Iran and never letting any chance to defame and isolate Iran politically. The Saudi Arabia's worries about Iran's influence undermine former's stance of role as a leader of the Muslim Umma.

- Besides the Arab states' opposition of Iran, Israeli has been among the largest part of choral accent alongside the nuclear ambitious Iran. In order to earn international support for its stance over clandestine Iranian nuclear program, Israel has explicitly and frequently slandered Iran's rise of military power. For Israel, a nuclear capable Iran poses serious threat not only to Israel but also to the rest of the region. Israel also termed Israel as a common enemy of the Israel and the West since its proclamation of intolerance of the civilized world that constantly struggle to tackle the anarchic attitude of the rogue states to undermine the global peace and security. For Israel, the threat of militarily strong Iran has exceptional repercussions than merely the issue of terrorism at the hands of pro-Iranian militias like Hezbollah and Hamas.

- The grave situation for Israel could outstandingly erupt in face of Iran having more political influence and economic superiority that however, as proclaimed by Israel will further fuel and contribute towards the rise of terrorism and the anti-Israel sentiment in the region. Once it comes to guiding principle, conversely, Israel suffers at a general impasse having lesser options where to tolerate a threat of Iran having nuclear capability. Otherwise, a diplomatically successful Iran bargaining leniency in the result of successful negotiation with the P5+1 powers over its alleged nuclear ambitions can subdue Israeli efforts to isolate Iran in the global political arena.

- The world is still facing the adverse economic effects of the war in Iraq, the Libyan conflict and the civil war in Syria. These wars have created a deeply disturbing humanitarian crisis in shape of refugees and food shortages. People in these affected areas are trying to settle in other peaceful regions thus creating flux of asylum seekers and illegal immigrants trying to reach Europe, Australia and even America. This situation is thus forcing these western states in different continents to spend more on their internal surveillance and border security measures that have a continuous recurring cost for the economy. Thus, another conflict or a nuclear weapon capability in the hands of Iran could just create the right conditions that could have devastating implications for the regional and global economy.

- The deal on the issue of nuclear safeguards of Iran with the IAEA will not be a major obstacle in Iran's path towards the peaceful use of the nuclear technology, which is its basic right under NPT. Apart from the peaceful use of the nuclear technology, the moves for the transformation from civilian to military purposes will never be an easy task for Iran. It is also one of the difficult tasks to anticipate about the nuclear programme, whether it is for civilian purposes or military purpose.

- The Iranian nuclear program has remained in the attention of West even after breaking out the controversy, especially with the revelations about some of the secret Iranian nuclear installations. Iran had been trying to reach an agreement on damage control by signing the additional protocol and allowing IAEA the access to these sites, situation however changed with the election of hardliner President Ahmedinejad in 2005. Meanwhile, the government not only refused to ratify the additional protocol but also stirred some further controversies by giving provocative statements about Israel that were strongly criticized by the Western world. Most of the states, including that of Israel, presumed that if Iran is on the road to acquire the nuclear weapons that they could then use to wipe Israel of the world's map. However, the assumptions of rogue Iran based on the faulty information and the deliberate misinterpretation have been instigated and propagated by the Western media against Iran. The controversy however, did evoke a strong response from the Western world that resulted in diplomatic condemnation and imposition of UN sanctions. These sanctions were in addition to that already imposed by the US government in 1987 under President Regan's administration and further tightened in 1995 by Clinton government. The US government added further Iranian companies and businesses to the existing list of sanctions that had adverse effects on the Iranian economy. Despite that, Iran had always maintained that these sanctions neither would hurt Iran nor would compel it to change its course on the nuclear issue; the reality appears to be somewhat different. Not only these sanctions seriously affected the Iranian economy, it also brought flexibility on the Iranian stance over its nuclear issue, especially after the change of the hard line government since 2005, which finally resulted in the successful signing of the interim nuclear agreement between the P5+1 and Iran.

■ Iran had been under severe economic sanctions and the sustenance of any nuclear program for the military purposes will need exceptional financial resources. Iran is one of the rich country in term of natural resources like oil and gas, which can add more cash to its treasurer through exporting surplus oil and gas while developing nuclear technology for its domestic needs.

■ The oil and gas trade are important tools of Iran's economy therefore, the increased wealth circulation through natural resources will align Iran in terms of economic and security bounds with neighboring and extra-regional powers and multilateral organizations of the world. Furthermore, financially stronger Iran could have a huge impact on the region. Tehran wants to acquire nuclear technology for two main purposes, one of which is the civilian use of technology for its energy sector and the other purpose could be for the military use of nuclear technology, most probably in nuclear bombs. The Sunny dominated Middle Eastern region is a very hostile region for Iran, where security arrangements are very complex and dynamic. Iran has enemy like Israel, which has monopoly over the nuclear weapons in the region. Arab States use every political and strategic move to enhance their influence to limit and counter Iran's influence in the region. The new era of relationship with West and the Russia enables Iran to play exceptional role in the milieu of international political, economic and security affairs.

■ In the regional milieu, Israel is equally belligerent state of Iran similar to the Arab states. Since Israel has already gained nuclear capability, therefore, a nuclear-armed Iran will increase the risk of a nuclear exchange because the militant groups like Hezbollah, Hamas and Islamic Jihad etc could feel emboldened to launch more active operations against Israel. The conflict could provoke a reaction from any side with brute force ultimately resulting in hundreds of civilian casualties and could provoke Iran to use the nuclear weapons as a justifiable mean to punish Israel. It was primarily the efforts of the European states and the flexibility shown by the newly elected much softer Ruhani regime which resulted into finalization of the interim nuclear deal with Iran. The successful deal would exceptionally increase Iran's political, economic and military influence in the region.

■ In case of militarily powerful state of Iran, her reputation or view as a Shiite state having a competing ideology is a threat and symbol of constant fear for Sunni regional monarchies. This scenario would definitely strengthen the Iranian regional stature that seeks aspirations from its old historical legacy. Such dominating power in the region could encourage Iran to promote its old ambition of exporting the Shiite influence form outside its borders through proxies, an aim that was set forth by the Iranian strategic planning in the region. This could further escalate the rivalries between the Shiite and Sunni states thus impacting the whole region. Such a situation would incite tensions among other states especially Pakistan, Bahrain and Saudi Arabia etc.

■ The other states in region including Iraq, Qatar, Lebanon and Yemen etc, are already facing the worst affects of this deepening sectarian rivalry, would plunge into chaos. Syria, for example is already in the middle of a civil war that is raging between the ISIS and the government forces, ruled by an offshoot of the Shiite split group. The spillover effects of Syrian civil war are already visible in Turkey, whose relationship with Iran deteriorated over the latter support to Syria, Jordan, which saw some of its own massive street protests, Lebanon, where sectarian bombings are gathering pace with the passage of time. The rising sectarian violence, not only risks initiation of a regional war but would also fuel tensions within other Muslim states inside and outside the region. The ideological differences of two hostile entities i.e. Shia Iran and the hardliner Arab world besides their exceptional wealth and the political and military power further drag the region in an unending race for power. The support for their ideology promoters in different countries will also destabilize the domestic and regional security situation of those countries.

■ Although, the risks are relatively less but after the recent US–Russian tensions following the Ukraine issue, the possibility of a regional war becoming a global nuclear war cannot be entirely ruled out. The world once again is shifting from the Unipolar geopolitical global order to multipolar global order in which other power centers like China and Russia are emerging which could physically get involved in the regional conflict and take definitive position like they took on the Syrian issue recently.

■ In the aftermath of the interim nuclear deal between Iran and the P 5+1 nations, the issue apparently looks to be easing out. However, if a concrete formula is not sought to peacefully resolve the problem of increasing influence of Iran in the region, a military solution might be considered either by the US or Israel as the only viable option to resolve the issue which could involve China and Russia in the conflict as well. Any Iranian retaliation on Israeli nuclear installations could invite a nuclear strike by Israel against Iran that could have devastation consequences for the whole world. First, the response of regional Muslim states could involve military retaliation due to public backlash or due to spilling over of radiation effects and second, a nuclear strike might push the global powers to physically intervene in the conflict which thus has risks of further escalating into a global nuclear conflict.

■ The divert views elaborate these sanctions not only proved to become a source of increased dilemma that drastically raised the cost of living in

Iran, thus adversely affecting the Iranian middle class, but major bulk of population since the imposition of sanctions after 2005. Therefore, these sanctions did affect the Iranian decision making process and the hard line stance on its nuclear issue. In the domain of clandestine efforts, portrayed as Iran is not the only country in the world that is trying to acquire nuclear technology through its underground efforts. Instead there are many other countries in the world that are also trying to acquire the nuclear weapons in the secret. Iran which was opposing the great powers' policies and threats forcing it to abandoned its nuclear porgramme. The ineffective role of the United Nations to safeguarding the rights and ensuring their security against any threat or use of force is also one of the driving force behind acquiring nuclear power status in the current international anarchic system. The anarchic nature of international politics promotes further anarchy and provides all the rebellious states for an excuse to protect their interests through any means, which also include the use of the nuclear weapon technology for its survival and security.

■ The integral analysis of Iran's quest to fortifying its military might to challenge the regional balance of power indicatives the fact that Iranian clergy has a keen interest in the gaining military superiority in the region. In the realm of developing nuclear program, the prevailing situation and the conclusion of the nuclear deal will set an example for all the states in the world particularly those interested to acquire the nuclear weapons at any cost. The exceptional secret measure in high benign environment to carry out its nuclear ambitions with being disclosed to the international community and IAEA in today world is impossible due to the technological advancement.

US-IRAN NUCLEAR DEAL: POWER DYNAMICS FOR IRAN AND SAUDI ARABIA

- The Arab countries already perceive threats through Iran's role in the Gulf and the Middle Eastern region by supporting militia and other non-state militant groups therefore; Arab countries feel their interests on stake. The threats of regional instability would definitely arise on the fronts when all the regional states will follow their respective agendas and interests without caring for the preserving the regional peace and security However, aforementioned threats are of major importance but at the same time it revealed the notion that, the acquisition of the nuclear weapons is not an overnight task to done with it. The development of the nuclear weapons requires a massive scale technical and physical labor to attain a nuclear capability. It also requires the huge involvement of technical and financial resources.

- The countries around the world are acquainted with the fact that the nuclear weapons are engulfed with gigantic consequences and the nuclear weapons are not too easy to fire. However, one cannot rule out the possibilities of the use of the nuclear weapons and such probabilities compel one to think about the consequences involved in it. Israel has also a track history of being the first nuclear state in the Middle Eastern region. Is pursuance of nuclear weapons capability was to endorse its influence upon other members of the region. Israel, in its nuclear program exercised a policy of ambiguity and opted for the virtue of caution and constraint as a unique feature of their nuclear program.

- The feature of nuclear caution in the form of a strict policy and a policy of nuclear opacity is Israel's most original contribution to the nuclear. The Israeli dominance remains wedged to their stance of maintaining a policy of continuity and opacity for their nuclear program that has distinguished Israel as a special proliferators' among the global nuclear club. It is an established fact that things keep on changing with every turn of a globe, and especially in the nuclear paradigm. Similarly, Israel has administered to certain challenges and difficulties with the growing recognition of its nuclear business that lend Israel to modify its policies to counter them. Furthermore, the compliance in the policy change accredited to Iran's nuclear program. Contrary to the Israeli case, the Iran's nuclear program demonstrated robust indications that a new nuclear order loomed on the new horizon, which induce certain repercussions not only for the region but also beyond it. The course of implications of emerging from the probabilities of politically and economically strong Iran poses direct existential threat to Israel. The set of implications leans Israel to modify its fundamental nuclear dogma. According to Israeli analysts, the prospects of patronage of proxy powers, Iran poses threat in a way that Iran has a determined and vigorous quest of promoting militias and the excessive hostility of the Iranian regime against Israel raises real concern among the Israelis. The sphere of influence relating to Iran's quest for regional hegemony provides a rationale for Israeli's confidence pointing that Iran's intentions and aspirations directed towards creating an auxiliary balance of power against all of its adversaries.

- The threat of war with Iran by Saudi Arabia and its allies war had gained credence in last few years but it appeared subsidized gradually, especially after the successful interim deal between Iran and the P5+1. Initially, Russia and Turkey struck the deal due to intense diplomacy from the European side and subsequently supported across the globe. The apprehensions regarding the Iranian nuclear intentions remained shrouded in mystery, as it could never be proven that Iran was interested in developing the nuclear weapons. The Iranian intentions regarding its nuclear program remained a contested issue between the analytical discussions viewing it as a quest for survival, especially after the US invasion of Iraq.

■ The other perception described as an Iranian strategic lever used for maintaining regional hegemony and global recognition, some believed it to be a national symbol of scientific advancement and development, while few considered the Iranian nuclear program an icon of national prestige used by the theocratic regime to justify and strengthen its rule. The Iranian used the nuclear diplomacy in an extremely successful way to gradually achieve not only regional stature but tangible economic benefits as well. Although, some statistics reveal that it was actually the successful approach adopted by the US President Obama to use stick and carrot policy towards Iran and thus imposing crippling economic sanctions which finally broke the Iranian will to defy international pressure and also paved the way for the less hardliner government in Iran.

■ The consensus on whether the Iranian nuclear issue has military dimensions or is just for sake of using as a diplomatic tool is also difficult to achieve and may actually vary from regime to regime in Tehran. During the times of Ahmedinejad, the strong and inflexible position adopted by the regime strengthened the apprehensions that probably Iran would ultimately move in the direction leading towards acquisition of the nuclear weapons. However, with the election of moderate Hassan Roohani, the Iranian stance and position over its nuclear program, especially with regards to enrichment of uranium has soften to a great extent thus paving the way for a nuclear deal, which although at this stage remains interim in nature.

■ This deal however, has built the confidence not only in Washington but also in Tehran that finding a peaceful solution to this problem through negotiations and talks is possible. Despite the interim agreement, the Iranian nuclear program viewed as source of continuous concern and a potential threat by Saudi Arabia have repeatedly opposed Iranian nuclear program and some have even gone to the extent of suggesting the US to stop Iranian nuclear program even if it entails surgical military strikes. Such a schism has badly affected the Iranian relationship with the Saudi Arabia. The strain in the US–Saudi relations is the manifestation of the US softness towards Iran, especially after the emerging situation in Syria and Iraq. Because of easing of relations between Iran and the West, Saudi Arabia become disillusioned from the Washington and are looking for defensive measures outside the protective umbrella of the US. Consequently, the GCC state view emerging regional Iranian stature and improving of its relations with the west, a source of concern which thus warrants special defensive measures. These states therefore are now looking for either purchasing the defensive equipment or are trying to seek shelter or nuclear umbrella of the nuclear weapon states. The media speculation about the possibility of Pakistan–Saudi nuclear collaboration also attributed to these developments in the region.

■ The concerns of Saudi Arabia is about the expansion of Iran's political influence in the region and its impetus for the nuclear weapons is much greater than the success of the nuclear deal between Iran and the P5+1 powers. The Arab league , which represents the interests of Arab states are skeptic about the nuclear proliferation in the Middle Eastern region, The Arab League is more concern about the currently existing security arrangements and the nuclear weapon free zone of Middle East than European Union and the USA.

US-IRAN NUCLEAR DEAL: POWER DYNAMICS FOR IRAN AND SAUDI ARABIA

- The nuclear-armed Iran or a powerful Iran with peaceful nuclear program is therefore likely to gain regional significance and global recognition which would tilt the regional balance of power in Iran's favor. Therefore, the Iranian role in the regional affairs and issues could have decisive say that would encourage other states to seek their own nuclear programs or regional arms race. This situation would exacerbate the regional sectarian tensions, especially in those parts of the region where Shiite and Sunni proxies are already engaged in fighting each other. Syria, Iraq and Lebanon are likely to see more unrest and violence in coming years possibly followed by spillover effects to other states like Egypt, Saudi Arabia, Bahrain and Yemen etc. Such a scenario could have a cascade effect for nuclear proliferation as states that situates in troubled regions of the world and have deep security concerns, like South Korea and Japan could think of developing the nuclear weapons amid growing Chinese and Russian influence in the region.

- The Saudi Arabia is one of the major actors in the region and the relations of Iran with Saudi Arabia viewed as open rivals in the Gulf. The Saudi Arabia being an ally of the US share overwrought sort of relations. Iran is challenging Saudi Arabia in its sphere of influence through proxies and non-state actors. The nuclear deal is disturbing balance of power in the region. According to one of the European Union's representative Mohherini, that Iran nuclear deal is moving in right direction and bringing some positive changes to the region. She further told to the officials of a high level committee in a meeting that International Atomic Energy Agency has confirmed the measures taken by Iran to properly implement Joint Comprehensive Plan of Action. She also urged the involving countries to work on successful implementation of the deal and its parts one by one. It is hoped that the successful implementation of deal would also be very helpful in solving all other outstanding issues of Iran with other regional and international actors.

■ The Iranian nuclear deal has considerably reached a momentous level of usual consensus for many other states other than the Arab countries. Besides the Arab states, the concerns of Israel are also one of the main pressing issues for the strongest pro-Israeli lobby in the Washington. The repeated threats to Zionist state from the Islamic Republic for complete elimination and wiping out from the world map are perceived as core threats to the very existence of the Israel. Along with Arab states of the region, Israel also shares a common concern about rise of Iran's military might and sphere of influence through provocation of proxy militant groups.

■ Moreover, the accustomed expressions about Iran-Israel relations besides the harsh circumstances were on the threshold of escalating into an open military conflict on numerous occasions. Likewise, to the situation viz-a-viz Arab-Iran relationship, the Israel-Iran relationship has been also a victim of historically repeated enmity and bitter experiences. The international efforts for the resolution of the enduring crisis have demonstrated exceptionally complicated for the reason that quite a few detach and the frequently disheveled and unpleasant course of actions took place at the national, regional and international levels. At the domestic political level, there was less chance for a roll back from typical stances against each other.

■ In case the interim nuclear deal fails to achieve the desired objectives and the peaceful solution towards the Iranian nuclear crisis would probably, lead to the military escalations in the region. Such a possibility would create a deep crisis for the whole world as the oil prices could climb massively and the oil supplies could be disrupted thus shaking the already fragile global economy to its foundations. States feeling unease from thought of a nuclear-armed Iran could heavily invest in the arms deals that could result in cutting expenditures in other important sectors like health, education, power generation etc, thus affecting the overall economic growth. The issues of less flexibility and ineffective diplomacy amidst intra-state relationship of the both sides never paved the way for a point of common consent. In general, the nuclear issue further added up to the predicament for almost all the stakeholders and the states particularly perceiving threats from the Iranian side.

Recommendations

- A politically stable Iran having sound relationship with the major powers of the world and living with a sanction free economy can ultimately play an exceptional role in the regional political, economic and security matters. This will automatically turn the fate of Iranian people with increased chances of better employments and earning and living with better standard of life as compare to the other nations in the region however, it demands increased cooperation of Iran with the international community. Contrary to that, a politically isolated Iran with nukes having position to pose existential threat to Israel and many nations in the West and even the security of Arab states on stake would put it under seriously challenging situation. Meanwhile, the European states are particularly concerned of the nuclear proliferation issue in the Middle East. Being in close proximity, they realize that in case of an Iranian's nuclear weapon, the tensions in the Middle East would rise which is already passing through a delicate stage and thus would affect the regional stability that could have drastic implications for the already ailing economy. The US and West polices towards Iran should draw the country away from the path of belligerent behavior by offering incentives and opportunities of trade and cooperation for regional and international peace.

- In 1929 during the Raza Shah Pahlavi's era, Iran and Saudi Arabia sign the treaty of friendship, which was the beginning of diplomatic relations between both countries since the establishment of Saudi Arabia. The relations of Iran and Kingdom were not as much friendly since its inception due to some bitterness rooted in their history. The King of Saudi Arabia arrived to Tehran in 1966 with his intended policy of strengthening relations with all neighbor countries and to bolster the political ties between different countries of the region. In the decade of 1970s, It was the matter of great concern for Saudi Arabia to have a competitor in form of Iran in the its immediate neighbor, who was constantly increasing its political and military strength and occupying different Island claimed by UAE. Immediately after the Iranian revolution in 1979, the Premier of Iran and religious clergy were critic of Saudi Royal Family. King Khalid was sending the message of goodwill gesture and Islamic solidarity for enhancement of relations between both countries. In Iran-Iraq war Saudi Arabia increases its oil production for financially support of Iraqi government against Iran and urges other regional states for the same to address the challenge of Iranian growing influence and military power. The incident of warplanes in the airspace of Saudi Arabia in 1984 and Hajj incident of 1987 further escalated the tension between sectarian divided countries. The incident of Iraq attack on Kuwait in 1990, brought two nation close to each other, but it was a temporary alliance and did not work for much longer. In the years 1998 and 1999, the relations of both countries improved with the agreement for increasing bilateral relations and increasing economic, cultural, and sports ties and visit of President of Iran Mr. Muhammad Khatemi respectively. In his five days visit , he discussed many important issues including security arrangements in the Persian gulf and oil production. Such agreements and visit can improve the relations of both states.

- For a prosperous position in the region, Iran has to show flexibility in order to grab the advantages possibly turn the destiny of this Islamic Republic. Though some hardliners in Iran still oppose the deal and consider nuclear program of Iran as sole right of the nation. Such elements oppose the discriminatory nature of the NPT and criticize that the treaty on the grounds that it equally does not bind all the states whether nuclear on not may abandon their program and possession of nuclear weapons. However, otherwise all the states may be given the right to carry on with their nuclear capability objectives at least for the peaceful purposes. The issue still prevails with the question that the states who acquire nuclear technology for civilian purposes can eventually divert it for the military purposes as well.

■ In the age of inter-dependency, it is important to resolve the Iranian case. The stance of the United Nations Security Council at some point reflects delicate position for allegedly having a role of enforcement agent for American policy preferences particularly in the case of Iran. The opposition is particularly pointed on the criterion that the nature of Security Council is not a suitable place to resolving the Iranian nuclear crisis. The United Nation Security Council has very few options on the table regarding Iran nuclear issue. The main purpose and desire of Iran nuclear programe is to deal with the Saudi Arab and Israeli in case of aggression against Iran. The surety of Iran' security is very essential to deal with Iran nuclear issue. The more recent usage of the doctrine of Pre-emption attack by United States of America against Iraq further fuels the idea of acquiring the nuclear weapon. Iranians will consider this to counter any great power aggression. And this great power aggression is also one major reason that many states are seeking the nuclear weapons.

■ Acquisition of resources (financial and military) and political power in the regional is playing important role in enhancing the capabilities of Iran through its non-state actors, which are apparently increasing the role of non-state actors in the region. Since the fateful events of September 11 and the role of non-state actors has acquired a new dimension in the international politics. In the Palestinian– Israeli conflict, the resistance groups like Hamas, Hezbollah, Islamic Jihad and Palestinian Front etc are more embolden with the post nuclear deal Iran which have more resources and less pressure from the international community. However, such a situation would also conceivably pressurize Israel to take the Palestinian issue more seriously and sincerely think for the resolution of this half a century old conflict that has become the enraging source of terrorism and instability in the Muslim world.

- Most of the conflicts in the Middle Eastern region are under the umbrella of Iran and Saudi Arabia. The rivalry between these two countries have created many battle fields in the region. It is also a fact that Saudi Arabia and Iran are interdependent on each other for current security arrangements in the region. Both countries are situated in a very less integrated and very volatile region of the world , which can escalate the situation with even a small incident. Many other emerging groups of militants mainly from Shiite sect could emerge in the Sunni ruled countries which could thus result in Sunnis forming militant groups of their own and thus there could be a sudden flux in the activities of non-state actors in the whole region. Even Khamnei reaffirmed the commitments to support Iranian proxies and allies in the region and proclaimed to always support the oppressed, Palestinian nation, Yemen, Syrian, Iraqis, Bahraini and rightful fighters of Lebanon. Saudi Arabia and Iran are not happy with decision of Obama administration nuclear deal that is feeding elements of instability in the region through treasure of Iran. Although State Department spokesman John Kirby denied any repercussion of this deal on the prevailing security situation in the region but there is need of concrete steps by P5+1 to include provision in the nuclear deal to ensure that the interests of others regional states will not be harm from Iranian side. It will not only ensure the safeguard of interests of regional states but it will also guarantee peace in the Middle Eastern region. The major reasons of bitter relationship between Iran and other neighboring states particularly Saudi Arabia is because of sectarian and ideological differences which never let the two sides to cooperate with each other and overcome the issues and commonly shared threats in the region. So there is a need of Confidence Building Measures (CBMs) to reduce tension and avoiding a security dilemma and crisis between Iran and Saudi Arabia.

REFERENCES

Abulof, U. (May 2014). Revisiting Iran's nuclear rationales. *Palgrave Macmillan International Politics* , 404-415.

Arnold, S. (2014). Peter Oborne and David Morrison. A dangerous delusion: Why the west is wrong about nuclear Iran. *Asian Affairs*, *45*(2), 343–344. doi:10.1080/03 068374.2014.910992

Al-Saud, F. b. (2003). *Iran, Saudi Arabia and the Gulf: Power Politics in Transition.* New York: I.B. Tauris & Co Ltd.
Ansari, Ali M. 2006. *Confronting Iran.* 1ˢᵗ ed. New York: Basic Books.

Blockmans, S., Ehteshami, A., & Bahgat, G. *EU-Iran relations after the nuclear deal.*

Burr, W. & Byrne, M. *Iran's Nuclear Program - Then and Now.*

Bardes, B., Shelley, M., & Schmidt, S. (2014). *American government and politics today.* Boston, MA: Wadsworth/Cengage Learning.

Barzegar, K. (2010). The Balance of Power in the Persian Gulf: An Iranian View. *Middle East Policy* ,74-87.
Berti, Benedetta and Yoel Guzansky. 2014. "Saudi Arabia's Foreign Policy On Iran And The Proxy War In Syria: Toward A New Chapter?" *Israel Journal of Foreign Affairs* 8 (3): 25-34. doi:10.1080/23739770.2014.11446600.

Broad, D. E. (2010, 1 2). *The New York Times Company.* Retrieved 5 5, 2015, from The Newyork Times Website: http://www.nytimes.com/2010/01/03/world/middleeast /03iran.html?_r=3&pagewanted=1

Burchill, S. (2009). *Theories of International Relations.* New York: Palgrave Macmillan.

Burhanettin Duran, N. Y. (Winter 2013). Islam, Models and the Middle East: The New Balance of Power following the Arab Spring. *PERCEPTIONS* , 139-170.

Bahgat, G. (2006). Nuclear proliferation: The Islamic republic of Iran. *International Studies Perspectives*, *7*(2), 124–136. doi:10.1111/j.1528-3585.2006.00235.x

Ben-Meir, A. (2009). Nuclear Iran is not an option: A new negotiating strategy to prevent Iran from developing nuclear weapons.*Digest of Middle East Studies, 18*(1),74–89 doi:10.1111/j.1949-3606.2009.tb00108.x

Bhat, M. M. A. (n.d.). "Religion" versus "rights": Why we are wrong about "defamation of religions."*SSRN Electronic Journal.* doi:10.2139/ssrn.2126822

Bowen, W. Q., Moran, M., & Esfandiary, D. (n.d.). *Living on the edge: Iran and the practice of nuclear hedging*

Chan, Maritza. 2016. "Non-Nuclear Weapons States Must Lead In Shaping International Norms On Nuclear Weapons: A Practitioner Commentary". *Global Policy* 7 (3): 408-410. doi:10.1111/1758-5899.12342.

Cohen, N. E. (Ed.). (2010). *Nuclear ambitions and issues in the middle east.* New York, NY, United States: Nova Science Publishers.

Cheney, R. & Cheney, L. *Exceptional Implementation of the Iran nuclear deal.*

Cooper, A. (2011). The oil kings. New York: Simon & Schuster.

Daniel Byman, S. C. (2001). *Iran's security policy in the post-revolutionary era.* Santa
       Monica: RAND.

Doyle, T. E. (n.d.). Kantian non-ideal theory and nuclear proliferation. *SSRN Electronic Journal.* doi:10.2139/ssrn.2551525

Dupont, P. (2013). Compliance with treaties in the context of nuclear non-proliferation: Assessing claims in the case of Iran. *Journal of Conflict and Security Law,* 19(2), 161–210. doi:10.1093/jcsl/krt017

Ellner, A. (2013). British nuclear non-proliferation policies towards Iran and the Middle East Cambridge Review of International Affairs, 26 (1), 225–251. doi:10.1080/09557571.2012.734780

Elasrag, Hussein. "(Gulf Security In Light Of Nuclear Deal With Iran)". *SSRN Electronic Journal.* doi:10.2139/ssrn.2709999.

E G Tan, E. (2016). The Iran Nuclear Deal: Containment or Appeasement?.RSIS.edu.sg. Retrieved 16 March 2016, from https://www.rsis.edu.sg/wp content/uploads/2015 /04/CO15096.pdf

Einhorn, R. *Preventing a nuclear-armed Iran.*

Maryland: Rowman & Littlefield Publishers.

Einhorn, R. & Nephew, R. *The Iran nuclear deal.*

Elasrag, H. (Gulf Security in Light of Nuclear Deal with Iran). *SSRN Electronic Journal.* http://dx.doi.org/10.2139/ssrn.2709999

Entessar, N. (Summer 2009). Iran's Nuclear Decision-Making Calculus. *Middle East Policy, vol. 16 no. 2* , 26.

Entessar, H. A. (1993). *Iran and the Arab World.* London: Macmillan.

Entessar, N, & Afrasiabi, K. (2015). *Iran nuclear negotiations* (1st ed., p. 133).

F. Gregory Gause, I. (2010). *The International Relations of the Persian Gulf.* Cambridge: Cambridge University Press.

Fiedler, Radosław. 2016. "Searching For A Nuclear Settlement. European Union Nuclear Settlement with Iran". *Przegląd Strategiczny*, no. 9: 51. doi:10.14746/ps.2016.1.4.

Forouzanfar, M. H., Goghary, J. S., & Daryabaygi, M. (2014). How can citizens take part in administrating a city? Case study: Sirjan , Iran. *Kuwait Chapter of Arabian Journal of Business and Management Review*, 3(12.a), 116–123. doi:10.12816/0018852

Flanagan, P. & Wall, C. *Coping with U.S. export controls and sanctions, 2015*

Fawcett, L. (2013). *International Relations of the Middle East.* Oxford: Oxford University Press.

Friedman, G. (2015, 3 31). *Stratfor is a geopolitical intelligence firm.* Retrieved 5 25, 2005, from Stratfor: www.stratfor.com/weekly/middle-eastern-balance-power-matures

G, N. B. O. (2012). The treaty on the non-proliferation of nuclear weapons and the challenges of nuclear capability projects in Iran and North Korea. *African Journal of Political Science and International Relations*, 6(5),. doi:10.5897/ajpsir12.028

Griffiths, R., & Yadlin, A. (2013). *Can the world tolerate an Iran with nuclear weapons? The Munk debate on Iran.* United States: Not Avail.

Gyngell, A. (2009). Writing the unthinkable: Narrative, the bomb and nuclear holocaust.Opticon1826. doi:10.5334/opt.060903

Hassani, M. 2016. "Iran Oil Production, Investment Policy, International Sanctions And P5 + 1 Deal With Iran, 2006-2015". *Contemporary Review of the Middle East.* doi:10.1177/2347798916664615.

Herzog, M. *Contextualizing Israeli concerns about the Iran nuclear deal.*

Herzog, M. (2015). *Contextualizing Israeli concerns about the Iran nuclear deal* (1st ed., p. 36). Washington: Washington Institute for Near East Policy.

Hitchcock, M. (2016). *Isis, Iran, Israel: And the end of days.* United States: Harvest House Publishers,U.S

Hicks, K., & Dalton, M. (2017). *Deterring Iran after the nuclear deal* (1st ed., pp. 114- 115). Washington, DC: Center for Strategic & International Studies.

Hossein Salavatian, A. S. (2015). Iran and Saudi Arabia: the dilemma of security, the balance of threat. *Journal of Scientific Research and Development* , 141-149.

Iran Overview. (2016). Worldbank.org. Retrieved 1 March 2016, from http://www.worldbank.org/en/country/iran/overview
IMF Country Report 15/349. (2015) (1st ed., pp. 15-19). Retrieved from (http://www.imf.org/external/pubs/ft/scr/2015/cr15349.pdf

Jahner, A. (Spring 2012). Saudi Arabai and Iran: The Struggle for Power and Influence in the Gulf. *International Affairs Review* , 37-50

Jahner, A. (SPRING 2012). SAUDI ARABIA AND IRAN: The Struggle for Power and Influence in the Gulf. *INTERNATIONAL AFFAIRS REVIEW* , 37-50.

Jafarzadeh, A. (2008). *The Iran threat: President Ahmadinejad and the coming nuclear crisis. New York: Palgrave.*

Jefferson, J. (2005). The unthinkable revolution in Iran; Charles Kurzman. *Digest of Middle East Studies, 14*(1), 109–112. doi:10.1111/j.1949-3606.2005.tb00890.x

Kimberlee, R. (2012). Stop, thief. *Neurology Now, 8*(5), 32–33. doi:10.1097/01.nnn.0000421660.65672.3a

Kittrie, O. F. (n.d.). How to strengthen the interim Iran deal. *SSRN*

Electronic Journal. doi:10.2139/ssrn.2356923

Kemp, G. (2001). Iran: Can the United States do a deal? *The Washington Quarterly, 24*(1), 109–124. doi:10.1162/016366001561582

Kahl, C., Dalton, M., & Irvine, M. (2012). *Risk and rivalry*. Washington, DC: CNAS.

Kaye, D. D. (2015, 4 9). *https://www.foreignaffairs.com*. Retrieved 5 5, 2015, from Foreign Affairs: https://www.foreignaffairs.com/articles/iran/2015-04-09/dont-call-it-shakeup

Katzman, K. (2016). Iran Sanctions (1st ed., pp. 29-33). Congressional Research Service. Retrieved from https://www.fas.org/sgp/crs/mideast/RS20871.pdf

Khan, S. (2010). *Iran and Nuclear Weapons: Protracted Conflict and Proliferation* . New York,: Routledge.
Latham, Michael E. 2011. *The Right Kind Of Revolution.* 1st ed. Ithaca: CornelUniversity Press.

Liedman, Opinion: Iran Nuke Deal Will Spawn More Proxy Attacks Like The Ones In Yemen, 2016

Lewis, O. (2015, 4 3). *Thomson Reuters News Agency.* Retrieved 5 5, 2015, from Reuters: http://www.reuters.com/article/2015/04/03/us-israel-iran-framework-idUSKBN0MU0BR20150403

Lina Haddad Kreidie, V. B. (November, 2013). The Rise of Iran:. *International Journal of Liberal Arts and Social Science* , 150-168.

Lerner, M. (2008). Iran with no nukes. *Tikkun, 23*(1), 11–12. doi:10.1215/08879982-2008-1005.

Mac Farquhar, N. (2012, 3 4). *The Newyork Times Company.* Retrieved 5 6, 2015, from The Newyork Times: http://www.nytimes.com/2012/03/05/world/middleeast/iran-elections-deal-blow-to-ahmadinejad-and-the-presidency.html?_r=2&nl=todays headlines&emc=tha22\

Maloney, S. (2016). *Iran Reconsidered: The Nuclear Deal and the Quest for a New Moderation*(1st ed., p. 69). Washington, DC: Brookings Institution Press.

Mazzetti, M. (2007, 12 3). *www.nytimes.com*. Retrieved 5 7, 2015, from The Newyork Times: http://www.nytimes.com/2007/12/03/world/middleeast/03cnd-iran.html?_r=2&hp&oref=slogin&

Menashri, David. 2014. "Iran, Israel, and the United States: Regime Security Vs. Political Legitimacy". *Iranian Studies* 47 (2): 367-371.doi:10.1080/00210862.2013.860329

Mousavian, S. H. (2014, November 27). *Why geopolitical shifts dictate nuclear deal with Iran*. Retrieved July 13, 2016, from Editorial, http://www.al-monitor.com/pulse /ru/originals/2014/11/iran-geopolitical-nuclear-deal.html#ixzz4FsLD5WT8

Mousavian, Seyyed Hossein. 2012. *The Iranian Nuclear Crisis*. 1st ed. Washington, D.C.: Carnegie Endowment for International Peace.

Milani, M. (2015, April 19). *Iran's Game in Yemen*. Retrieved May 5, 2015, from www.foreignaffairs.com: https://www.foreignaffairs.com/articles/iran/2015-04-19/irans-game-yemen

Mannully, Y. T. (2009). U.S.–India nuclear cooperation and non-proliferation. Nuclear Law Bulletin,2008(2), 926. doi:10.1787/nuclear_law-20085k9gw7rzmlhd

Miller, J. (2008). *Iran*. Washington, DC: Center for a New American Security

Nader, A. (2015). *The Impact of Sanctions Relief on Iran* (1st ed.). RAND Office of External Affairs. Retrieved from http://www.rand.org/content/dam/rand/pubs /testimonies/CT400/CT442/RAND_CT442.pdf

Norell, M. (2015). A really bad deal: the Iran nuclear deal and its implications. *European View, 14*(2), 285-291. http://dx.doi.org/10.1007/s12290-015-0365-3

Parisi, R. & Esfandiary, D. *An EU strategy for relations with Iran after the nuclear deal.*

Parisi, R. & Esfandiary, D. *An EU strategy for relations with Iran after the nuclear deal*

Patrikarakos, David. 2012. *Nuclear Iran.* 1st ed. London: I.B. Tauris.

Porter, G. *Manufactured crisis*

Pietrobon, A. (2013). Nuclear powers' disarmament obligation under the treaty on the non-proliferation of nuclear weapons and the comprehensive nuclear test ban treaty: Interactions between soft law and hard law. *Leiden Journal of International Law, 27*(01), 169–188. doi:10.1017/s0922156513000587

Rajiv, S. (2016). Deep Disquiet: Israel and the Iran Nuclear Deal. *Contemporary Review Of The Middle East, 3*(1), 47. http://dx.doi.org/10.1177/2347798916632324

Robert Einhorn, R. N. (2016). The Iran Nuclear Deal: Prelude to Proliferation in the Middle East? *FOREIGN POLICY AT BROOKINGS* .

Rosenberg, C. B., & Fox, P. D. (2013). Leveraging the trade preference program to secure a state's compliance with international law obligations. *The Journal of World Investment & Trade, 14*(6), 1009–1018. doi:10.1163/22129000-01406005.

Samore, Gary. *The Iran Nuclear Deal: A Definitive Guide.* Cambridge, MA: Report for Belfer Center for Science and International Affairs, August 3, 2015.

Saudi Arabia: Putting on a brave face – Analysis. (2015). Eurasia Review. Retrieved 14 February 2016, from http://www.eurasiareview.com/14012015-saudi-arabia-putting-brave-faceanalysis/

Stone, R. (2015). Iran deal would transform its nuclear infrastructure. *Science, 348*(6231) , 164-165. http://dx.doi.org/10.1126/science.348.6231.164

Schwartz, P. N. (2015). *What the Iran Deal Means for Russia.* Washington, D.C: CSIS.

Sebenius, J. & Singh, M. (2013). Is a Nuclear Deal with Iran Possible? An Analytical Framework for the Iran Nuclear Negotiations. International Security, 37(3), 52-91. http://dx.doi.org/10.1162/isec_a_00108

Sheikh, S. R. (2015, 3 29). h*ttp://www.globalresearch.ca/unholy-alliance-between-saudi-arabia-and-israel-a-us-iran-nuclear-deal-would-trigger-regional-political-re-*

alignments/5439349. Retrieved 5 6, 2015, from The Global Research website: http://www.globalresearch.ca

Stone, R. (2015). Iran nuclear deal opens door to scientific collaborations. *Science*. http://dx.doi.org/10.1126/science.aac8844

Secretary, O. o. (2015, August 5). *www.whitehouse.gov*. Retrieved October 10, 2015, from https://www.whitehouse.gov/the-press-office/2015/08/05/remarks-president-iran-nuclear-deal

Salus, B. (n.d.). *Nuclear showdown in Iran: Revealing the ancient prophecy of Elam*.

Schneider, M. B. (2013). Has Iran covertly acquired nuclear weapons? *Comparative*

Strategy, 32(4), 308–312. doi:10.1080/01495933.2013.808108

Sokolski, Henry D and Patrick Clawson. 2005. *Getting Ready For a Nuclear-Ready Iran*. 1st ed. [Carlisle Barracks, PA]: Strategic Studies Institute, U.S. Army War College.

Sagan, Scott Douglas and Kenneth N Waltz. 2003. *The Spread Of Nuclear Weapons*. 1st ed. New York: W.W. Norton & Co.

Skancke, J., & Friedman, L. (2010). *Iran* (1st ed., p. 69). Detroit: Greenhaven Press.

Spying on the bomb: American nuclear intelligence from Nazi Germany to Iran andNorth Korea (2007). *Choice Reviews Online, 44*(06), 44–3473–44–3473. doi:10.5860/choice.44-3473

Stevens, C. T. (2014). *Iran S nuclear program sanctions Reli*. United States: Gazelle Book Services.

Samore, G. & Allison, G. *Decoding the Iran nuclear deal*.

The U.N. Resolutions | The Iran Primer. (2016). Iranprimer.usip.org. Retrieved 11
    December 2015, from http://iranprimer.usip.org/resource/un-resolutions

Tarock, A. (2016). The Iran nuclear deal: Winning a little, losing a lot. *Third World*
    Quarterly, 37(8), 1408–1424. doi:10.1080/01436597.2016.1166049

Thakur, R.(2012). To stop Iran getting the bomb, must we learn to live with its nuclear\capability? *Strategic Analysis*, 36(2), 328–334. doi:10.1080/09700161.2011.6465 U.S.-Iran nuclear deal could shift regional power. (2016, April 10). Retrieved June 02, 2016, from http://www.lfpress.com/2015/07/19/us-iran-nuclear-deal-could-shift-regional-power-balance

Unthinkable: Iran, the bomb, and American strategy (2014). . New York, NY, United States: Simon & Schuster Children's Publishing

Yafai, F. A. (2013, 8 6). *The National is a multi-platform news organisation.* Retrieved 05 25, 2015, from The National:http://www.thenational.ae/thenational conversation/comment/hostility-between-iranians-and-arabs-betrays-history

Yazdizadeh, B., Majdzadeh, R., Alami, A., & Amrolalaei, S. (2014). How can we establish more successful knowledge networks in developing countries? Lessons learnt from knowledge networks in Iran. *Health Research Policy and Systems*, *12*(1), . doi:10.1186/1478-4505-12-63.

Zak, D. (2016). *Almighty: Courage, resistance, and existential peril in the nuclear age.* Bloomington, IN, United States: Blackstone Audio books.

Zetter, K. (2015). *Countdown to Zero day: Stuxnet and the launch of the world's Firstdigital weapon.* United States: Broadway Books (A Division of Bantam Doubleday Dell Publishing Group Inc).

ABOUT THE AUTHOR

Sajid Mahmood Khan is a Graduate in Politics and International Relations from Quaid-i-Azam University, Islamabad Pakistan with distinction. He is doing research on geopolitics of Middle-East. His research interests include contemporary politics of Middle East, South Asia and International Relations of great power. He has optimistic views with a touch of realism about the future of the world and peace within.